How to Find Success in Marriage, Relationships and Love

The Success You Always Wanted in Love, Marriage and Relationships

By

Raymoni Love

authorHOUSE

1663 LIBERTY DRIVE, SUITE 200
BLOOMINGTON, INDIANA 47403
(800) 839-8640
www.authorhouse.com

© 2004 Raymoni Love
All Rights Reserved.

No part of this book may be reproduced, stored in a retrieval system, or transmitted by any means without the written permission of the author.

First published by AuthorHouse 06/10/04

ISBN: 1-4184-2422-6 (e)
ISBN: 1-4184-2423-4 (sc)

Library of Congress Control Number: 2004093817

Printed in the United States of America
Bloomington, Indiana

This book is printed on acid-free paper.

Dedication

I will like to thank three important people in my life, whose faith has help, me to envision life as a writer. The first is my Uncle, George Sturgis, who gave me my first typewriter. The second is my Dad, Romalis, who presence was always felt in completing this book. Last and certainly not the least, Jennifer, who support is unequal, and without you, none of this will have ever been possible.

Table of Contents

Dedication v

Part I: Women, Are You Ready to Find Your Love Or Enrich The Love You Already Have in Your Life?................................. 1

    Chapter 1 His Past Is Your Future 3

    Chapter 2 What is Your Preference? 9

    Chapter 3 Understanding A 'Player'.........................17

    Chapter 4 Your Man, His Friends, His Family And You, His Woman..23

    Chapter 5 If You Cannot Talk As Adults 27

    Chapter 6 Why Another Makes Him Feel So Damn Good? 33

    Chapter 7 A Mother of All 39

    Chapter 8 You Have an Honorable Design 45

    Chapter 9 He's Not the Only One You're Hurting 53

    Chapter 10 A Meeting in the Ladies Room 57

    Chapter 11 Many Women Wish They Were You.......75

Part II: Now Men Are You Ready to Find That Special Lady Or Enrich The Love That Is Now In Your Life?...................... 83

    Chapter 12 Her Past Is Your Future............................85

    Chapter 13 A Lady and Her Opposite 93

    Chapter 14 She Can 'Play' Your Ass As Well As You Can 'Play'

Hers 101

Chapter 15 Your Woman, Her Friends, Her Family And You, Her man 107

Chapter 16 A Father of All 113

Chapter 17 Understanding, Can Be Hard To Come By 121

Chapter 18 Why Another Makes Her Feel So Damn Good? ..127

Chapter 19 Cooperation and Understanding: Measuring Your Manhood...133

Chapter 20 Men: Everything Will Be Alright 139

Chapter 21 There is a Meeting in the Men's Room 147

Chapter 22 Many Men Wish They Were In Your Shoes 161

Part I:

...Sorry Men This Part is for The Women

Women, Are You Ready to Find Your Love

Or

Enrich The Love You Already Have in Your Life?

His Past Is Your Future

Chapter 1

The determination of what type of flower we will become depends on the seeds that are sowed. Many of you women do not believe that delving into a man's past is important, just long as they respect you and treating you right. However, you have to explore one's past if you want to have a healthy and successful relationship.

Now, you cannot judge a book by it's cover, I believe you heard this before, because people do change. Nevertheless, in order to understand what the meaning of the book you have to read it, and if the conclusion of the book is not palpable to your taste, at least you can put it back on the shelf. This is the interrelated structure of life, and this is the code of many relationships, is to shelve what is not needed.

However, we have to keep in mind, people do change, either for the good or the bad, but they do change, and once you become involved with someone, you just cannot put them on the shelf like a book you read. Because a relationship is centered around two individuals (unless *there are children involved*) and when you decide to end any relationship, your feelings is strongly affected like the man you are getting rid of.

This is why understanding your man's past, would inoculate you from any nonsense or abuse that might resurface when his emotions are high. Many of us love being in love so much that we sacrifice many essentialities just to make things work. Society donned enormous pressure on males to succeed, however, handling the pressure is not the male's problem, not having auspicious parental guidance creates pressure, and a problem all on it is own.

A man cannot give the right love to anyone, if he does not understand what the right love is. A mother is the first to give a child love, and the mother is the first that the baby loves. Unfortunately, many children are devoid of this kind of love, and it sometime, actuates them to divest from assimilating into a normal and moral society.

In addition, in their quest to be normal or accepted, they find themselves running down life's spiral and intricate roads, just to wind up psychologically impaired. Love can cure many things, accept a mind and heart that is obdurate, and hate filled. It would take more than love to cure a mind with no conscience; it would take a Supreme Being.

Today, many of you women find yourselves in situations where you are questioning your man and their behavior. It is apparent that many of you women want love and to be treated right, but just cannot erase the fact that your man is behaving like a damn fool.

A male child not reared in a positive family atmosphere has a deeper pain than the ones that does. Now I do not mean they are inferior or degenerate when it comes to intelligence and social skills, oh no! It just means they love different, and sometimes it may take awhile before they truly and sincerely show it. They are apprehensive, because everyone, whom they ever loved, did not love them enough, left them or took them for granted.

In addition, their behavior may reflect their concealed hurt and disappointment. Nevertheless, they still can love, and as they grow into adults, their hearts always will question love, and the giver of it. So, when you find yourself dating a man with a trouble childhood, keep these things in your mind.

His relationship with his parents is extremely important when it comes to the development of your relationship. However, children being reared in homes with honor conveyed to them understand that it is imperative that they give it to their own family and relationships.

Beautiful women please listen, understand, majority of men has a 'panic' room inside of them, just to control, and hide from unwanted dangers. See, women in order to find the right man, you have to thoroughly and honestly understand yourself and what you will tolerate. A man is what he is, and that is a man, and he needs to be respected as one.

In today's society, there is a big misconception when it comes to relationship and who should be in control of them. With the emergence of women in politics, education and employment, women have certain ideals that convince them that they can live without a man, by the way, many men carry themselves, and I agree with them in many ways.

However, as long as there is love, a woman with a PhD., a woman who is a CEO, a woman who is a glamorous singer or teacher in a classroom, still is need of it, and strongly requires it from a real man. Sure, many women can pay their own rent, purchase their own vehicles, and have their own money, and some can even intimately satisfy themselves.

Nevertheless, there is a need in every woman to have a man, in this book, you will understand the man you need, and what kind of man you want. See; in a man's past, you will learn if he wants someone to provide for him, or if he wants to be the provider.

Here I am sitting in a Coney Island on a day I suppose to be at work, however I needed this scenery cause everyone here has a tendency to deliberate on the conditions of their relationships. There is a person here explaining to another about how his woman constantly nags him. Moreover, he has to kick her ass from time to time just so she can behave correctly.

Any man in his right mind, knows, that it is wrong to put his hands on any women. Somewhere in his past, he must of witness his father or mother's boyfriend beat on his mother, just to bring a solution to their disagreement?

Love is kind, love is compassionate, love is sincere, and having a man hitting on any of you women, it is not love he is expressing, but acts of rage emanating from his trouble childhood.

Violence permeated my childhood and adult life, and no, I am not talking about me being the perpetrator. I have seen women and men in violent relationship, and their fear of being alone is leaving them with a foolish excuse of accepting it. I understand it is hard finding another companion, but what they fail to realize, is that your life can be taken away, and you'll still wind up alone somewhere in an unmarked grave.

In addition, the fact remains for violent men and women, anyone succumbing to violence to solve their problems is only adding to them. Everyone strives for acceptance and this enable them to reach for the highest in employment, sports, and life. However, if you are reaching for the highest fulfillment in your relationship with your man, you will need the sincerest cooperative understanding of his past from him.

If you are developing deep feelings about a certain man, in your future, understanding his past will inculcate you on whether it will be a happy future or a traumatic one. If you date a man and you early detect that he has characteristic of jealousy and possessiveness, save yourself the trouble, and leave him alone. Jealousy is a sign of weakness, and possessiveness is indication of control.

You do not need to be controlled or trapped in any situation to be loved. You have your own mind, and it is sweeter to have a woman who is willingly giving herself to a man. Ladies make him understand you love him, make him understand that you are with him and with him only. If he does not get help for his jealousy, frightening temper, or any kind of abuse, and then move on. I know you believe you are worth more than what a careless man offers.

Ladies, you are the strength of a man; you can give him joy, a family and infinite happiness. Love your man; love his imperfections (if he is willing to correct them) because we all have them.

However, everyone must reach for the highest heights in life, and having a thorough self-examination, can one truly achieve greatness in life. Help your man correct his problems, and have him to help you correct yours as well.

When two are in a boat and the ocean seems endless and stormy, complaining about who is paddling the most is not going to get you to your destination. When life becomes stormy and problems seem endless, individuality is not what makes relationships. Hold on to one another, and never lose faith, then you will discover that life's storms are only temporary, but love in it's purest form is everlasting.

What is Your Preference?

Chapter 2

When one comes of age, what kind of companion they will like to attract is always on their mind? Imagine a situation where you are out with your friends and you see some handsome man standing near looking back at you; what is the first mature thought that comes to your mind? Could it be "…is he cute enough, he dresses impressive, is he attractive to me, or is he available?"

Life is about choices, and whatever choices you decide, you have to live with, but how long, are up to you. Every man cannot win a popularity contest, however, what is best for you are extremely important, and the only thing that matters. In this chapter, I will expound on three men who have vastly different personalities, goals, and aspirations. In the end, you will decide who is most befitting to share your world. Therefore, are you ready

Raymoni Love

for the man behind curtains number 1? Well he can be found internationally, his aspirations are naught, so he is classified as a bum. I can classify him as a bum, because I am a man, and a man can view his peers as he sees them. He is a man, who willingly gave up on life, so he fails to attain positive goals, so he succumbs to 'do nothingness'.

Life is not easy, and although we all have choices, the same string of opportunity that measure a man successful, measure a bum as a failure. Many men cannot have that beautiful house on the hill, and unfortunately, many cannot be that proud doctor or lawyer. However, striving to achieve success in a way that is positive for our world is the measure of any man.

I know there is many of you women, who had men who started out on the positive economic side of life, then fell off. Instead of getting up when down and brushing him self off, he acquiesces, and become accustomed in his new economic status, and this is why I called these men bums.

A bum is an individual who gives up when things are bad, and chooses to be left alone in the mire of poor economic status. He wants a woman, however, for all the wrong reasons. I know many of men who are bums. They live at home with their parents; they have no job and could not keep a job if they had one. Some of them are good for something, cause I see many of them with good beautiful women. See, I know you women can't help being easy persuaded when a man put that loving down on you, but getting caught up with a man's sexual attributes blind you to a reality in which you cannot determine if he's right for you or not.

Children are to be raised, not grown ass men. Sure some of them may need a little help, however, if a man does not want a job, and do not

How to Find Success in Marriage, Relationships and Love

take care of his responsibilities as a man, than your help is vastly being taken for granted.

I been in situations where I was from job to job, and the pendulum of my economic status was swinging on many depressing lows, however I refused to succumb to life's disproportionate lows, and I just couldn't digest the idea of being taken care of as a man. I always believed that helping someone is good, but helping yourself is beneficial for your own development.

In addition, I tell you another thing that disturbs me, and that is I just do not believe that it is a good thing for a man to beg or ask profusely another man for spare change. I understand that society creates a gulf so the have-nots have a hard time finding a bridge to prosperity, because when life unfortunate conditions knocks you down, society tries everything in its power to keep you down.

Imagine being homeless, and the only place that will accept you is a shelter, the shelter is funded by donations from people who have spare change to give. It cost more to house a homeless person annually, than it does to give a man a yearly income. A man without positive role models or direction gets punish for stealing food, and with no mercy, he goes to preliminary exams and mockery trials, then the state imprisoned him. It has already cost taxpayers $70,000, or more to imprison a man for stealing a $10.00 steak.

Then he is released from his incarceration, in the exact predicament he was in before he was hungry. If a state is paying $30,000 to house a criminal, how much do you think it will cost to rehabilitate him with a job and a decent place for him to lay his head? Nevertheless, this is a choice; men must get up and face their conditions, so they can provide a positive contribution to other disadvantaged men, and their world.

Ladies, a man is suppose to love you right, and a man cannot have you and should not want you if his priorities are not in order, because without his priorities in order evokes stress, depression and frustration. So, if you want to be loved unconditional, have your man, yes, the one with no job and stay at home with his parents or he may live with you, recondition his moral and self-esteem and get his life on the right track.

Hanging out with his friends doing drugs and alcohol with your money is not going to make him a better man. They say the lord hates a coward, well a man who does not work and is not educating him in school or college is a man who is afraid of life, in other words a coward, and in plain English, a bum.

Now let us move on to the thug. Many women are attractive to thugs, a.k.a. ruffians, a.k.a. violent person, and a.k.a. lawless person. What ever your preference is, like I mention before is up to you, however, thugs are deviants of a system of morality. They have there own solutions when it comes to dealing with life's unfortunate reoccurring problems.

A man does not have to belittle himself by being a non-conformist, if he is willing to stand on the side of justice, then his only obligation to non-conform to any and all systems that separate him from doing right.

Some of you women may have a man who sells drugs for a living, okay this is fine, many drug dealers are not strangers when it comes to jail or prison. Prison or jail may release you on their terms, however society does not grant forgiveness or immunity from your man's nefarious past. Society does not understand rehabilitation; they only understand what your man was, as they watch him through a magnified glass for your man's next criminal offence.

No one enjoys being under a scope all their life, but society fails to understand that it created this poison in our lives, and the people in power have not the decency to apologize. Selling narcotics is a wrong that many of us men have no choice but to do. Sure, we may need money to feed our family and ourselves but it is wrong, and feels terribly sorry for having our backs against life's positive wall.

Many men who sell drugs are unfaithful, as many of you women have discovered. See the drug game only brings temporary happiness, which is filled with violence, strip clubs, and women and limited success. See, many of you women are attractive to money that you will sleep with any man who looks established enough to help you with whatever problems you may have.

The new cars and fine homes, you women are so attractive to, however, you sleep with the idea every night that your man is unfaithful, but go along with it because you do not want to lose that car or house. Then reality sets in, one day that drug-dealing boyfriend does not come home, he is either gunned down by jealous men or arrested, facing a large quantity of prison years.

I do not blame people who sell narcotics as much as I blame the system that produces them. Drugs are wrong, and selling drugs just to reach a certain end, is a decision that is dragging many of our men imperiled.

Drugs destroy families and neighborhoods. Drugs are a hell that is so hot that even the softest whisper seems like a scream. Mothers on drugs, having babies on drugs is the wettest tear God can cry.

In addition, any women who want to be involved with thugs and other deviants of a just society, this is your business, just keep in mind you are creating a world where love and happiness is a temporary high that attract negative people, insincere people, jealous people and depraved people. Involving your self with a man who fails to follow the honest and moral roads of life is saying so much about yourself.

Sure, men have to do certain things to make ends meet, but if they can find other means that do not imperil their lives, I surely would appreciate it and you will to in the end. There is no longevity in being a thug or a criminal. Some where in a man's life, when he obtain a chance to live a whole fulfilling life, he must ask himself, have I love completely, and have I made the supreme being proud.

Ladies you only live once, and putting your life in jeopardy, riding around with thugs with no direction, must remember forgiveness is never acquired when your mouth is infinitely shut to ask for it from some graveyard. If you want love and harmony, then here is your chance here is your choice right here, and he is considered a 'real' man.

He has a job, his own place and direction. He loves completely and he honors his woman in his life. I am not talking about those superficial brothers who think just because they have a good job and have that nice car, that they can treat a woman any way that they can. Oh no! I am talking about the men who value love and are committed to preserving it, a man who will not jeopardize your life with foolishness and unlawfulness. A man who takes cares of responsibilities with his children, a man who understands a woman's feelings and respects them. A man, who respects society, but is committed to effacing its imperfections. A man, who knows that satisfying his woman, starts with her mind and heart, not through her vagina. A man who honors God by doing the best he can in an honorable way. A man who is not afraid to pray with his woman, and enjoy living with his woman, A man who truly understand that he has one life to live, and want to share it with one woman, with one love, with one direction and with one God.

So women, you have your choice, there are many good men in this world, can you be the right one when it is time to hold one?

Understanding A 'Player'

Chapter 3

You are out on a date with a person who has potential to be in your immediate future. He opens the door for you, he stands by your chair before you sit down, and he compliments you on your looks and attire. He laugh at your sense of humor, he has no problem spending money on you, he makes you feel like you are the essential part that has ever entered into his world.

His phone conversation have your hopes and dreams back on track, then all of a sudden, the thought of Mr. Right permeates your mind. Now your body is eager to see if he can please it so you decide to see if his 'package' is good as his manners, and whether it's good or alright, anxiety clouds your mind with such disquiet feelings that you wonder if you did the right thing or not.

So far so good, he calls you after exploring your lovely body, than all of a sudden, something just seems to good to be true. As your quest take you to numerous of uncertainties, you discover that you are not his only girl, and the decision to be kept or dismiss is in his power, because you know a man sometime thinks with his penis. Therefore, the woman with the sweetest vagina and unforgettable sex is the one who will get the rose.

You feel used and dumfounded, and your heart is the only muscle in your body standing on pure honesty, as the conclusion presents itself, in which your heart already disseminated to you, yes baby, you been 'played'. Your emotions are passed the Richter scales, while all unnecessary thoughts cross your mind. You want to confront him, but afraid his sweet talk might land you back in his bed. You want to hurt him like he has hurt you, and lied to you, but Judges are giving long prison sentences so that particular thought quickly fades. You listen to love song after love song, as you pull the pillow underneath you so it can catch your tears, and as the teardrops land on your arm and pillow, you blame yourself for everyone that falls. While at the same time, blaming you and accusing yourself for being stupid, while also paraphrasing the words so many heartbroken women always say, "I am through with men".

When one is searching for true love, sometime one can become so naïve to the lies that appears to be so blatantly true. Heartache is a pain many of us try earnestly to avoid, but having a sincere spirit, one enters a zone where trust is on the threshold, but wrong is on the throne. In addition, through life has clouded tunnels you realize the wrong, which give you that vitality to move on.

When a man has a hard penis, his thoughts are solely on the woman who can help him release his backed up 'juice'. I loved playing the field, and my conquest from woman to woman has left many women hurt and disgusted. Thanks to Solomon (you know the great king in the Bible?), man's journey to express his masculinity with numerous women dates back to the beginning of time. David who is Solomon's father, had a penis that was so erected, that he set up Uriah to be killed, just so he could have Uriah's wife, this is an indication, that men will go through many things just to see how good a woman's body make him feel.

In today's society, sex is a determination for success of any relationship. Sometime men, who have been hurt, act out their discontent, by playing with women's hearts. Like I indicated before, I loved playing the field, however, by me being a conversationalist, I just love exploring different women's minds. It is not right, but in order to find the right woman, someone's feelings have to be affected in a beautiful way. My sexual appetite led me to become intimate with different women of many different nationalities almost every day of the week.

It's vitamin to a man's ego when he learns he can satisfy a woman, because many men today exhausted their will in satisfying their women (oops that is in chapter 2, in the book, What is wrong With My Woman?), and you know this is why many of you cheat. However, commitment is a gigantic step, and if that step leads you on a journey where many of you women are deceived and hurt, so what! The dating game is the survival of the fittest, while the 'player's' game is the survival of the slickest.

Sex appeal is the first thing that crosses a man's eye, whether you have a nice ass, nice breast, or nice lips, you women have a gem that immediately attracts a man's eye. A 'player' has many reasons why he find attractive in women, like for instance, he might be attracted to her lips, because to him, "it's nothing like having sex with a woman whose sexy lips are on his @#$! %*.

The art of having many women is all in a 'players' game, but it can become a very dangerous game. See, women who are hurt can become enraged, and try and damage a 'player's possessions, or she could let a 'player' have sex with her so she could call rape, or pretend that he impregnated her, or she could stalk him and make a memorable public scene. A heart that has been deceived is more dangerous than a fool with a gun is. Then you have some 'players' who'll inform you of their 'other' women, just so things like this are averted.

However, some of you just women still want your waters tested, cause you know a man is looking for the sweetest vagina, and the hottest sex, and you want to compete and become the highest bidder. However, wait a minute, having good sex is not the only thing, you must be drama free. Nonsense sometime can be entertaining, but not when it is clouding a 'player's game. Many men feel a way to a woman's heart is through her vagina, misconception or not, the tale is told that if you make a woman feel good all the other channels will open.

In today's world of up and down relationships, a way to avoid a 'player', is to become one. You cannot judge a fruit by the way it hangs from the tree, because when it is ripe or rotten, it still is some good to somebody. Meaning, games being introduced by a gentleman or 'player' is still some good to somebody, it just a matter of whom believes it more.

Becoming familiar with a potential man does require you to get to know him, long and thorough. If he wants your sweet sex, if he wants to see if you can arouse his mind as well as his penis than you need to let him wait it out. If he wants you that bad, give him a picture to masturbate on until you are ready to give him the real thing. In addition, when you decide to give him the real thing, make sure you understand the consequences if things are not what you expected. Let a 'player', a gentlemen or a rogue find the essence of your mind, and through this venture, he'll discover that lady who radiates with confidence, respect, beauty, honor and dignity, so he will have no other alternative but to respect you.

Your Man, His Friends, His Family

And You, His Woman

Chapter 4

There are numerous of problems that can impede the progress of a relationship, one of them is outside influences. I fervently believe that opinions that are not guided on wisdom and positive concerns should be silenced. You have your man and he is taking care of his responsibilities as a man, however his family and friends are in the mist of your relationship.

Every little girl wants to be the Cinderella rescued by prince charming. They want the type of dream man that everyone loves and honor.

However, fairly tales are only complete at the end, fairly tales are just what they are, fairly tales. See, every relationship goes through problems, and sometimes we need someone to share our problems with, someone who is less expensive than a psychologist and more honest than our families.

Your man may be close to his mother, and mom may not approve of you, neither one of you should let anyone put a stain on the relationship. He must be willing to ask his mother for advice, and if it is pleasant or negative he must discern it apply the positive to his life, and then move on with his life. Ladies please understand, when you try to impede the advice from the one person who is close to your man, you are asking him to give up confidant and later on, you will be asking him to give you up as well.

Sure, family should mind their own business; however, you are in love with their family, so it is their business, especially if he decides to put a ring on your finger. Yes, it may become rough along the road, and it will seem like they are questioning your sincerity and integrity, you must never put yourself in a position to abdicate your morals, if you are a lady, be one. Your self-respect will generate so much acclaim that just when they feel that they do not approve of you they will wind approving of you.

If his in-laws are like out laws, and some of friends are something like crack heads, never having the right thing to give, but always asking for it back. If your man does not disassociate himself from negative friends, what does that say about your man? Sure it is all right for him to go and hang out with his friends, however, he must separate his friends from his relationship. I know some of you ladies have someone who you can sit down and talk to whether it's family or friend, like I said before, if you are going to discuss private details of your relationship just make sure it is not going to be expensive.

See some people who you may consider a friend or maybe someone in your family you trust could be the one who will put all your personal business in the streets. A king will not jeopardize the success of his kingdom by consulting with fools, and your man should not jeopardize the success of your relationship by disseminating his personal affairs with people who does not have his interest at heart.

In addition, you should not interfere with his relationship with his family or friends, he is a grown man (at least I hope he is) he is capable of making decisions of his own. You are his better half, so if he is complicated with a problem you will be the first to know. Women please understand every man needs to get away from home for a while, you may not be to particular of his friends, but they are not for you to choose.

If there are children involved, it is great to have both families participating with the children, however, when it comes to welfare of the child no one should be closer than the mother and father. I some of you women have discovered, everyone wants to give advice on your child and how to raise it, I know this can difficult and painful. This is when you must put anyone one in there place, whether it's family or his family, if you are doing a good job with your children, than those outlaws need to find them some other business.

You are his lady, the pride of his life, you come first, and the families come second. Do not be that fool running around town trying to please everyone that she can, you will wind up destroying yourself and those hypocritical people will only say that you shouldn't have ran your self in the ground. Although we all know, they are trying to work you in their 'family'.

So, ladies remember you only go around this earth one time, give your man all the love that you can, respect his family and friends and you will discover, being yourself is wonderful a transformation. Remember ladies, there may some who does approve of your wonderful qualities, however, one day they will wish that they had them for themselves. Be the rock of your own family, your man, your children, and yourself, because through it all, this is where your love will be greatly honored.

If You Cannot Talk As Adults

Chapter 5

When laughter and intimacy is replaced with screams and 'fuck yous', you realize there is a problem. Everyone enters a relationship with an understanding that each day will not always bring blue and sunny skies. However, you proceed with the faith that you will extinguish any problems that may impede the success of the relationship, only to discover that what you are actually extinguishing is the communication that began the peace process.

You want to solve all misunderstandings, only to discover that in our misunderstandings, no one wants to be wrong. You reach a critical point where you are screaming and using vitriolic words, she's shouting just to talk over you, and before you know it, hurtful words and actions ensue, establishing a detrimental foundation that will always be remembered when you disagree again.

It is okay to disagree; it is just how you disagree which is important. When there are two people talking at the same time, who is doing the listening? There are several things, which can test the strength of a relationship foundation. Whether it is financial, instability, employment stress, or family issues, problems arise and adult situations cause for adults with understanding. Communication is what keeps love and understanding present in pressured situations; however, one must have the compassion to share it with the one they love.

In many relationships, you will always find someone who does not express him or her thoroughly, and this is where things become difficult. In my relationship, the smallest thing I would let worry me immensely. My woman would practically beg me to express what is on my mind; I would shrug her off and just reply that I was not thinking about anything. I wanted to tell her what was on mind, however, hurting peoples feelings have always came difficult for me to do. Than I learned, that honestly may or may not hurt the one in the receiving mode, but it would forever insult the one in the giving mode.

Does your woman have a difficult time expressing herself to you, or do you have difficult times expressing yourself to her? Ask yourself what is it that always has you and her at each other's throat? I will try to cover certain issues that have relationships on the rocks:

Your Words That Verbally Abuse Your Woman

I understand it can become difficult with your woman, who does not know how to respect you. In addition, there is nothing in the world so dreadful and demeaning than to have someone assassinate your character and positive attribute with hurtful words. Vitriolic words will live with you until you get Alzheimer's, and then you might not forget.

Gentlemen, our women are tired of being some man's bitch, some man's whore, and some man's tramp. Sure, we may find ways to apologize for using such words with our women, and may even throw a little sex on them to help clear their mind from the verbal abuse. However, when she does not come home on time, or she does not cook what you want, or she does not give you unlimited sexual pleasure, such as oral sex, then you'll soon rediscover that you're still a bitch or a whore.

Your Woman's Words That Verbally You

Now I know our ladies can tear our manhood apart with her tongue. When situations become incensed, that deduce verbal insults amongst you and your woman, we wonder how they find the words, however they must emanate from somewhere on the darkest side of hell. Words like, "motherfucker your dick ain't shit, that's why I'm not fucking you", "you are a sorry ass man, you can't fuck, you can't keep a job, and you're a punk ass motherfucker", and the list of names go on and on.

Now gentlemen, we must understand why common courtesy is so important. If you and your woman cannot talk to each other like adults with wisdom, then you should depart as friends. Majority of problems in relationships arise because honesty and genuine concern is not present. When financial problems surfaced, it will be best if the two of you handle the situations honestly and carefully. One you has talk, while the other one is listening and contrariwise.

Let's say a bill is due, and the analysis discover that someone is spending well needed cash on things that they shouldn't, like entertainment, or you might have spent some on your car, or you she be shopping when actually she should be looking like she is shopping. Understanding where the money is going and coming can give an honest appraisal when financial problems manifest their ugly heads.

Saying I Love You And Showing I Love You

When you love one another, saying it is an indication of truth. See, you can easily tell your woman that you love her, however, if you are not showing it than you do not love her. Action is a language all of it's own, and abuse is a language all of it's own. Showing humility and understanding when one disagree, is an indication that love is present, when communication and verbal abuse is used to explain things that proper English can, than is extremely important that adults put them in there proper places.

How to Find Success in Marriage, Relationships and Love

Gentlemen please keep in mind, you can go around this world telling everyone that you love them, however it will go in one ear and out the other. However, if you find a way to show them in their life that you love them, then the entry into their heart will not be denied.

Why Another Makes Him Feel So Damn Good?

Chapter 6

A box of Kleenex that is not enough to wipe away all the tears you have cried after you'd discovered your love has been unfaithful. There are no cures for broken hearts; cause broken hearts never mend when they can always remember. The saddest chapter of any relationship occurs when one decides to solve their discontent of their relationship by cheating. Why does he cheat? Lovers become unfaithful when things they cannot control become too serious for them to accept responsibility for.

A woman needs to look deep inside her and ask herself is she doing the right things to satisfy her man. Men are different when if comes to the qualifications of a female. Some want one with looks, some want a woman to be able to cook, some want a woman to be clean and some want a woman with intelligence (can you believe some men want a woman with a nice body, no matter how stupid she is?).

When a man finds a woman that appeals to their liking, they pursue her hopefully get her. Ladies, if you want to know why your man is cheating, or why he will eventually cheat, I will go over four detailed parts that will explain all you need to know on how to keep your man faithful and committed, unless you a 'player'. The first topic is

<u>Sex</u>

Sex is extremely important when it comes to a relationship, satisfying each other can open many doors that will eventually lead to some happiness. Some of you women have put your men on pussy rations, I know you women understand what I'm saying, see when you feel your man has been a 'good boy', then you give him some sex, any other time you become to tired and have an headache.

However, men love oral sex, so ladies if you feel you're out of practice then if you want to keep a man you better get back in the habit and give him some oral sex. However, do not be afraid to tell him how you want it, see some of you get tired with the same old positions. Some of you want that vagina coughing up orgasms every chance it gets. And if your man need a little help, just tell him how you want than he wouldn't feel that you are keeping sex away from him, because now he understands either he satisfy himself by satisfying you

So ladies, lesson number one answer is: If you want to keep your man, make sure you give plenty of lovemaking, then he'll be too tired to stick his limp into another woman.

Missing Qualities

Every man love a woman whom they can respect, but what makes a man respect you ladies, is the way you carry yourselves. Some of my friends have women which did very little to keep their homes clean. It made them feel uncomfortable every time guest came over, however it was his woman, and without him advising her to be cleaner, he continued to create more misery for himself. I love a woman who look so good with clothes on that's what I would prefer, see, majority of you women have bodies that you are proud of, keeping that body fitted and fresh will always help you keep your man.

In addition, I do not know how many of you women cook, however, just a little magic in the kitchen will always keep your man stomach delighted and your body pleased. Societies have pervaded everyone with customs and fashions, however, intelligence is something required, and many of you women are devoid of it. Tell me ladies, who want a woman whose proper English is defined by the many vitriolic words she has spoken? Character is prerequisite when dealing with society, and a woman with wisdom can achieve more in life with her mind than with her body.

In addition, I still cannot believe we still have women in our society who still does not a thing about etiquette. Do you know how embarrassing it is to eat at a table that is not properly set, and do you how embarrassing it is to see a women eating with a fork she doesn't know how to hold? Perfection is not required, however, self respect permeates your lives ladies, so strive to be great within, then no man will have to look inside to define, cause it'll show on your face.

If some of you women are mothers, you have one of the respected jobs ever held, because your tender hands rub the head of the next President, King, Queen, or Emperor. We need you to continue and with little more help, raise our babies correctly and respectable, and we men will proudly assist you in any way you want us to.

Thanks be the glory to a woman who has a husband, you truly have been blessed. Some of you love keeping your husband satisfied emotionally and physically is your priority. No one is demanding anything from you, we understand that you all have these qualities inside you, and we just ask that you proudly bring them out.

<u>Physical Quality</u>

I understand that none of women are trying to become a Miss America, however, eating healthy and living healthy will keep your man healthy. See, I love a woman with a nice physical attraction, because this is what I am going to love to be entering at night, and women if your body are not right, how do you expect your men to respect and cherish it?

You do not have to over eat or under eat to keep a man, whether if you are big or small, love will find you, only if you are proud of your physical shape. With all the sexy clothes, they have on the market today, why not introduce your self to them. The reason I'm saying this is because when I'm out of shape, I feel bad and that evokes me looking bad, ladies you have all the right equipment, please put them to use before the rain of cancer, overindulgence and unhealthy eating rust them out.

Compatibility

Love is a special thing when one can share it with another; however, one must be willing to accept it in order for it to be appreciated. I know none of you women want your men to leave, however, if things are not right between the two of you, one of you are going to leave anyway. Sex is important, physical quality is important, and personal attribute dealing with quality is important, but if one is not compatible then you must correct the flaws and continue to love. I love a woman who I can communicate with, cause then I am confident that any misunderstandings we have will be resolved. If you feel that his childish play is not up to your standards, than I know plenty of women who will love to listen to that play all night why that hard penis is getting her wet.

If you do not like going out with him or spending quality time with him away from the home, then that woman who you thought couldn't get your man will. Sharing quality time together is extremely important, and he must be willing to sacrifice too, to keep your relationship amicable. Now you have an understanding of why your man cheat, all you have to do is follow these guidelines and he will be a good boy and stay home.

However, if he still wants to mistreat you and cheat, all attributes you have learned will be right and beneficial to your new man. Never stop loving, because one day that love is going to be accepted by someone who is going to truly and sincerely appreciates it.

A Mother of All

Chapter 7

When one is in love with someone, faults are ignored, love, and promise stays on the horizon. You love your man, you will do anything for that good man of yours, but what if he has children, does fold your hands, and not interact with them, or do you play step mom? When love is in it is purest form; negative intentions and negative people subside.

There is no such thing as a perfect relationship, however, as long as they have common sense, there will be no difficult problems, that would impede their quest to try to be perfect. Marriages and relationships do fail; the lost is dreadful and hurtful, especially when there are children involved. There are many single men with children, some are taking care of their responsibilities, and some are not.

However, the children of the world have been created, and they do have fathers (at least I hope they do). There is so much nonsense today with single fathers and their children's mothers and vice versa, that everyone just needs to take a chill pill. I know it can be stressful on your behalf when dealing with your man and his former acquaintance or acquaintances.

I am a man with children, and I usually do not bring my children in to any relationship unless I am married, because confusion can cloud a child's mind. We Men go through enormous problems with our baby momma's, and trust me, we 'real men' dread bringing you 'real women' into stressful situations.

However, you love us, but we create a problem that may complicate your life style, and that is we do packages, and those packages are our children. Ladies, we men of your lovely heart have tremendous pressure on us, and we truly appreciate your valuable commitment to us in our trouble times. Men, who have children from our former relationships, go through pressure of not visiting them or not having enough to provide for them. In addition, it hurts them deeply when they have to belittle themselves just to have a relationship with their children in the mist of all their you women nonsense.

A child needs a home, and if two people in love can give it to them, than it will be rewarding for the world. You can love your man and not be part of his children, because, honestly it is not your responsibility, however, is this kind of woman you want to be? A woman bogged down in individuality that she could not love something or care for something that is part of her man.

I was in the barbershop the other day, and I heard a woman talking about how she does not want a man with children. She said, "Men with children are a example of irresponsibility". However, this in many instances could be factual, and consequently, that woman has every right to express her ill feelings about men with children. In addition, she need not to limited herself, yes there are men with children, there are also some of you women with children who does not reside in the same home with your children's fathers. However, if we all disassociate ourselves from a child who comes from a broken home or dysfunctional family, how do we expect to brighten our tomorrows with laughter and harmony if everyone just stops caring for the ones who needs it?

Ladies, do not think of your self as a baby sitter, and do not lower your self to the games your man's children mother plays. Just focus on the commitment to making your man happy, and if you find your self, assisting him in the development of his children so be it.

In addition, I understand you have concerns about what happens if the relationship end, should your relationship with your man's children end. The thought of getting close to his children and all of sudden you cannot see them any more is painful to digest, it almost makes you feel like you were wasting time getting close to the children.

I was in a relationship where my girlfriend would help take care of my children, and although I had a child at the time with her, I really appreciate the love and care she gave to my children. Though we are no longer together, my children still ask how she is doing.

In addition, there are a vast number of children being raised in homes, where the parents who produce them, are no longer a pair. Everyone seems to be helping and raising someone's child. It is within us, to give love, but some time pride takes over, and has us to with draw it. Jealousy and resentment of one another is too much a burden to exercise our character.

Now a time will come when you might disagree what the child is doing or have done, however, and the question crosses your mental skies should you, or shouldn't you, discipline some one else's child? Children do not need to be abused physically or verbally, if you have to discipline anyone's child, you must make sure the father respect that you will do the right thing.

The children you shared your love with will remember for long as they can remember what you done for them. Many of the children you have raised will not come back and thank you for what kindness you bestowed, at least you know in your heart that you have love them and accepted them unconditionally. Trust me ladies, your contribution to a better future always start with the community and home contributing to the positive development of any child.

Adults are responsible to give a star-studded performance to every child, cause we are the heroes and heroines of a bright tomorrow and preserving the lives of all children. If we limited our concern, our love and our peace to just our immediate family, the whole world would all need to admit themselves to a family council. Being a mother to your child, to your man's children or child, is a gift that God grants to queens who are the preservers of his promise.

You Have an Honorable Design

Chapter 8

In the beginning, the purpose of a woman was to be man's helpmate. However, through the vistas of time, women your roles have become incredible and magnificent, as well as complicated. The road to your independence was not easy. However, through their desire to be equal, women you have courageously rose to the occasion in education, science and politics, despite opposition from people who felt that women should stay in there assign "place".

Although many of you women have achieved many things in life, there are still many of you that are lax and frustrated by the limitations yourself. Some of you women find yourselves struggling with your own inability to be great. Some of you women want to be that glamorous actress on the screen, the President of some successful enterprise, a highly decorated Doctor who daily saves lives, a wife who takes care of her family, or the teacher that teaches the children.

However, women some of you fail to understand that there is a calamity in being successful. Some of the women achievers I have mentioned reach their distinction, but had to overcome many impediments to be successful. Many of you women in the world, who feel that they are insignificant, or never reached their true goals, must understand the success of the world starts within.

There is a world within every one of us, and sometime the pith of our potential is only attain through proper preparation and true self-examination. Everyone can be great, everyone can be important. However, to be great, or to be important does not necessarily mean that your name has to be up in lights. Today there are many issues going on about the change in human rights, and at the center of these discussions is always the hot topic about abortion, and woman's right to choose.

The debate over women's rights is so complex; you have the President and people of religious sects segregating their beliefs and moral concerns. If you look around, everyone wants to be a consensus leader or person. Many people are thinking that if the majority is doing it then it must be right. When one find himself ignoring his personal convictions for the sake of being popular, then that person must question their ability to live. See, on the other side of life, there are a majority of physically dead individuals whose vain ideas are resounding in a ghostly whisper, saying, "Think before you follow."

I am not trying to step in the battlefields with abortion and antiabortion advocates. I am going into the battlefield of right, cause in the end this is where many wish they could be. Though man's laws and legislation are seemly contrary to what many of you believe, God's plan rest in the womb of all you women. Before I get deep into the discussion of life, let us meditate on the conditions of women who had to make such difficult choices. Women, many of you are going through life void of proper goals, and poor guidance and bad decisions is leaving many of you psychologically damaged.

You have a husband or boyfriend, but something is making you feel that your men do not love you or support you as well as you would like them to. Alternatively, you feel that you are being taken for granted and not getting enough love. Then some of you women just want to be recognized for some of the things that do, but no matter how hard you try, your effort goes unnoticed.

Women some of you question yourselves everyday of staying in relationships where abuse is present. Many of you women are in dire need of love, and through your desire to acquire true love, you start opening your legs to numerous of partners which also leads to no avail. Then some of you women on the job feel that if you flirt a little or use your female attraction, that you can be elevated to a better position. Last, you have women in church, which finds their souls standing on the line of heaven and hell, you want to walk right and do well, however, the pressure of the world is leaving them bewildered and confused. Women you need to remain strong, cause this will help you obtain that vitality you obtaining life's highest heights.

All you women have the ability to do marvelous things, but excessively loving a man, materials things and false friendship are distancing some of you from your ultimate goals, and that is being the pillar of strength your world, and your family needs. It is all right to love, but do not be blinded by it. Love is so beautiful. Love is the medicine that revives and heals a trouble sprit. If love can transform the human sprit, life can generate infinite possibilities.

When we are in love many of us engage in premarital sex. Understanding sex and its power, we must be able to accept the responsibility, whether we use protection or not. Women, who have the opportunity to carry life, you must not take this gift for granted. Abortion is taken life away and robbing everyone the chance to be blessed by a beautiful child presence. There are some of you women that wish you had the opportunity to give life, and it saddens you to see other women easily and conscience free destroying a life. Children are the embodiments of their parents, they have something of the father, and something of the mother, whatever it is; it makes all children beautifully unique. There is no excuse destroying a life you irresponsibly made while having a good time.

What should you do when discover that you are pregnant and not married? I will not try to undermine your choice, all I ask is that you consult her heart, and the question will answer itself. Being loved by a child that came from your womb is immeasurable when it comes to being loved by anything or anyone.

Men may leave you, friends may desert you, and employers may unfairly dismiss you. However, a life that you bring into this world is a priceless gift, and there is nothing in the world that can reach such an achievement. If you do not mind, I will like you to take a journey with me into the past for a moment, and witness the extraordinary things God has brought about through a woman's womb.

Let us clothe ourselves with the clothes of Hebrews slaves drench with God's tears, and listen to the cries of mothers, whose male children are being killed, because of pharaoh's fear of a deliverer for the Hebrews. Then vision the strength of one mother who saved her son from the wrath of pharaoh, whom would later become the man who holds tablets written with the hand of God, with instruction for all mankind to obey. Moses was that child who was given a chance. Moreover, with his life, he wrote a new definition for freedom.

Oh! Here is a man, who is the word of God in physical form. He healed the sick and raised the dead. His earthy mother and father were guided to a safe haven where the child would not be harm. You may call him King of Kings, Lord of Lords. However, he is the greatest of all that ever lived.

Then there is Harriet Tubman, who led many slaves to freedom. Franklin D. Roosevelt, a president who carried his country's problems on his poor health, and realize that America can only be great if all Americans stand together. In wartime or depression time, Franklin D. Roosevelt made changes to his presidency that all Presidents after him would emulate, and honor. In addition, there is Lyndon B. Johnson my favorite president, because I believe his heart was in people and social programs that enrich life and prosperity for all people, and he had the persuasion to make others that deplored his ideas believe in them.

Helen Keller, the little angel who witnessed the depravity of man, wrote of such horrors so the world could see how wrong prejudice is. Mahatma K. Gandhi, who use non-violence to win independence for his homeland, only to set a peaceful method, that would later be used by an American named Martin L. King Jr., who use it to change conditions many thought would be impossible.

I understand that it is hard raising a child with men, whose hearts is devoid of love and compassion. Be careful women of the men you have sexual activity with, if a child is created and feelings are not real, you do not need to be in a situation where you might have to abort a child. It is your choice, but if you understand sex is a part of creating and sharing true feelings, and if you cannot wisely refrain from having sex, then you should wisely keep the child if one is created.

It is a sad situation that we are in a society where killing is so acceptable. Emotions are high when a woman is pregnant, and depression may set in when she ponders that she is alone in her pregnancy. That is your child! That is your baby! No woman needs to appease any man or anyone when it comes to a decision of having a child. You need to please yourself by making a wise commitment when it comes to sex.

How to Find Success in Marriage, Relationships and Love

One day sit on a park bench and just look at the beautiful things that are exciting in this life. Sure, you might see some negative distraction, but this is what makes life even more beautiful. Because you have the ability to witness the sacrifices, many people have made just so you can be here breathing. Do you believe that your unborn child should have a chance to do great and wonderful things when it exits your womb? Good.

Just imagine their first step, first call, or the first time they laid their eyes on you. Yes, raising a child is not all peaches and crème; but do not give up, because things do get better. Through your womb, you are making him or her great, and with proper love and guidance, through their life, they will be making you great.

He's Not the Only One You're Hurting

Chapter 9

"I wish we could just get along," do you find yourself saying this after you and your mate have had a quarrel? Do you find yourself searching deep within for answers that will conciliate and renew your relationship? Alternatively, do you find yourself in a tug of war that has you pulling for a renewed love affair, while your man is pulling for a departure? Then there are those feelings that take you back when love was painless and little less complicated. You reminiscence about the time you dated and fell in love.

Raymoni Love

Your dreams of a beautiful home and family just pervade your mind that a smile unnoticeably appears on your face.

Then reality sneaks up on you, and love does not so love and a kind word seems to resonate as vile and loud signifying that your relationship has gone bad. When you are in bad relationship, and trying to fix something difficult with the wrong tools, you are asking for stress, distress, and heartache. However, when things are not going right in your relationship, there is unrelenting powers within that actuate you to go on. Relationships sometime can be a pain, and then they can be a joy. It is not so difficult to end a relationship when two people are just involved, but when children are present, many of us have not learned to walk away without vexation or vindictiveness. When I love you spoken by loving lips turns into I hate you spoken by vindictive lips, and with children witnessing the altercation, the altercation is no longer between adults. Children are the innocent little bundles of joy that are unfairly used to make any fight an unfair fight. Children can become uninviting guests in a terrible situation where their parents are expressing conniption and violence. Relationships sometime can be a quest down a road that leads to fulfillment or disaster.

Today's relationships consist of couples that have not learned to disagree, and this has become disastrous for the children. If fathers and mothers could display the same courtesy and respect towards each other when they were involved, then their children would still be reared with love, which is important to their development. The problem with mothers and fathers today is retaliatory responses. The mother's retaliatory response when a relationship has ended is to withhold the children from their fathers, and the father's retaliatory response is to stop providing and visiting the children.

Every relationship does not go through these problems, but in some way or another, everyone emotionally or physically express their dissension for broken dreams and a broken heart. Women you are lovely creatures who share man's rib, I know words cannot express how wonderfully it feels making love to your who is unconditionally in love with you.

Now women you all have a tendency when you are hurt to try to punish your man any way that you can. Yes, men do you women wrong sometimes, physically, emotionally, mentally and spiritually. This does not mean to keep their children from them when you are upset. Women you need to understand it is not only the man you are hurting but also the children. Women when you are hurt, it is obviously that you have many tactics to use to retaliate. See, many of you women will dishonor yourselves by having sex with someone just to get even with your man, or some of you women can become so incensed and withhold the children from their father's, or find means to procure their boyfriends and husbands income or both. However, everything becomes nonsense when you have two adults fighting and disrespecting each other and dragging the children into it. This is leaving our children neglected and psychologically impaired. Just because a relationship end, that do not mean you start treating your ex like never cared. Broken homes do not have to scar our children, just because you and your ex are not under the same roof does not mean you can raise your children together. Loving someone is a beautiful thing, but you can still love one another without making love to one another. Yes, men need to start taking more responsibility for their actions, they cry about wanting a family, children, and lovely wife, than turn around and maybe cheat on you or abuse you. Every thing is not perfect; every rainbow is beautiful but not eternal. Showing love to your former boy friends and husbands will result in one of the most beautiful chords ever played by a musician. Love men like you would want someone to love your sons and do no be blind or hypocritical. If you make love your regulating ideal, then you will be doing the world and our communities a great justice for your children's future.

In addition, women you need to find better ways of expressing your feelings when things fall apart in relationships. Some time men love you, and then turn around and do something to terribly wrong you. If you and your ex boyfriend or husband are having similar problems communicating or just getting along, maybe you and your man need to take a course in cooperation and understanding, because it is apparently clear that you to may not understand what it means to love and love unconditionally.

We have to keep in mind, children are the focal point of our lives, if we cannot show them that peace and understanding is the best thing to have, how can we expect them to build a world with these attributes?

A Meeting in the Ladies Room

Chapter 10

There are many women who are dissatisfied with the way their men has been treating them, and then there are those who are happy with their relationship with their men, and both women, the unhappy and happy, are confabulating their experiences in this chapter. Therefore, I have taken the time to travel, listened, and witness women from all over express in numerous ways their relationship and break ups with men. In addition, for all those who wish to express themselves more openly about their love, lost love and more and could not be part of this chapter, here are your colleagues

Raymoni Love

who also share your love and concern and wish to dedicate this chapter to you.

Dating

"The dating game can be frustrating sometimes, because you can spend all your time getting to know someone, then later on you discover that they are ass hoes. If men understood what they want out of life and from us, then the dating game would not be one of survival of the fittest." **Maria, age 46**

"Men ain't shit, I went out with a guy for about two weeks, and before I knew that he was married twice before, he wanted to marry me and sleep with me. I feel many women is jeopardizing the dating for us not whores and slut women, because you have these women sleeping with men before they know their last names. I take time to know who is gonna get my pussy, because my shit is to good to be given to a guy who do not have a job or respect for women." **Sabrina, age 27**

"Oh! I just love men and I love giving my body to men, however, I like for them to earn my loving, because I use to give my shit up to a man two or three weeks after taken his number. Then I have learned that men respect a woman more when she plays hard to get. Men can be funny sometimes, they want your pussy, then you give them a chance to get it, and then all of a sudden, they start acting like they are your father. If I could get less drama, more respect and romance then the dating game would not be so bad." **Mary, age 30**

"I am just tired of dating these stupid ass men who think just because they spend a few dollars on you, that a woman is suppose to give them some sex. Whatever happens to those days when it was great to date and fall in love. I would do anything if I could find one man who truly understands how a woman is suppose to be love." **Nicole, age 28**

"I dated my current boyfriend for about two months before we got serious, and although we had a few mishaps here and there, I can say I'm glad I fell in love with him. See I believe lot women make their mistakes at prejudging a prospective man before she takes time to understand him and his ideals. The dating game is like an interview, you have to ask all the right questions, and listen very carefully to all the answers, because somewhere in between, the real man you will get is waiting. **Marie, age 35**

"Me and my husband dated for about a month, and we became serious soon after that. My husband or boyfriend at the time I should say wanted to know what kind of love he needed to provide for me. He use to say, 'Gloria, I may want to hold you, I may want to make love to you, and I know I want to marry you, but if I do not know you and you do not know me, then everything we try is going to fail'. I love the way he was honest, and I love the he was patient for me. In the dating world today, many men are not so patient, they want to have sex with you, then children, and want

Raymoni Love

to shack up with you, without any idea of a woman's plan and feelings. See women need to focus on getting and finding a man with real love and plans, if more women put their concerns out front and their tender hearts in the back when it comes to giving information about them, then many of them would be married by now. **Gloria, age 32**

Giving Him Some

"My pussy is so good I tell you, men just go crazy over this shit I got here. However, this has been my major problem in dating. See I dated a guy for about two weeks, and we got so heated being under one another for so long I had to have his dick, and when I got it, I wish that I had not. That man just went crazy, I mean he wanted to know who was calling me, why I was late coming home, who was I going out with and everything. So I told him if you do not stop your bullshit, we are done. You what he told me, your pussy is too good to let anyone else have some, and threaten me that if I leave him, that he will hurt me and the guy I gave it up to. I am telling you ladies, be careful of the men you give your pussy to, because it could wind of being the last one you give it to." **Josie, age 25**

"I was with a man for about three weeks and I gave him some, it was good but it could have been better. I do not know what to tell you, am that I felt I was doing the right thing and we are still together and making better sex. I would tell women out there, that you have just one body, if start preoccupying their minds about safe sex, and who they are considering to please it, then men would have no other choice but to honor and respect them". **Jackie, age 30**

"I remember I gave a man some after a few weeks of dating, and he stop calling me for about a week. Then one day he pops up over my house wanting some more sex without explanation of where he had been. I am just tired of men and their games, I do not feel I done anything wrong. See I took the time to know him, and I even met his parents and children. Then I later found out why he was gone for so long, he was on the run from the police for being delinquent on his child support. I learn from that experience, that maybe women need to up the weeks of consideration of sex to about six months or so, if they truly want to know what kind of man that are dealing with. If he decides to be impatient and go and date someone else, at least you learn that he was not even worth your time, and now he someone else's problem now." **Tonya, age 21**

"I believe that getting to know someone is very important now that you have so many diseases. If a woman respects her body, then she would take responsibility in knowing and understanding who she share it with." **Sherry, age 35**

I Know there is Someone Who Loves Me

"I was in a abusive relationship, where every time I did not do what he said, he would strike me. I remember one time he almost killed me. I was bathing our son in the bathtub, and he kept calling me, but I could not hear him because the water was running. He charged upstairs and when I saw him, his eyes were almost like seeing the devil himself or something possessed. He then punch me several times and started putting my head in and out of the water in the tub, and if it was not for our son screaming at him to stop, I would not be alive today. I reported the incident to the police, and I filed a personal protection order against him. I do not care what anyone says, having a man kicking your ass, or verbally abusing you, is the closest thing to death. I would never in my life let another man put his damn hands on me again." **Stephanie, age**

"I am so glad God heard my prayers that day, because I could sworn I would be dead. I was sleep, and my husband was out supposedly having a good time with his friends. He came home screaming with liquor on his breath, talking about I slept with his friend Tom. He went outside into his car and came back with a gas container, he started pouring gas on the bed, and he held me down while he poured gasoline in my face. Then he screamed, 'if you want to fuck devils, then you need to burn like them!' I immediately jump up, and he set the whole room on fire, and I was screaming from the burning of my flesh, I managed to jump out the window and a neighbor who heard what was going on rescued me. My husband never made it out, the house and him was just enflamed. I do not understand why men find it possible to want to harm their women who they face everyday. My husband friend who supposedly told him that I slept with him was killed instantly when my husband heard the lie he told." **Beth, age 44**

"My boyfriend came from a family where abuse was always visible. Sometimes when he and I disagree, he would slap me across my face, and sometimes when we are having sex, he always forces his penis inside of my butt without lubricant, and he would slap me profusely if I screamed. One time I told his fried that he has a nice car, he slap me so hard that fell down and my head crack his friends car window. I could not hide the bruises anymore from my parents, so I told them. I wind up breaking up with him, I just wish I would have seen the physical damage my father and his friends did to him, I heard that both of his arms had to be reset." **Ann, age 19**

"I had to show my boyfriend that I did not play when I said ain't no motherfucker going to ever put his hands on me and live. One day he came in the house smelling like sex and perfume of another woman, and I question him about it. He kept telling me to shut the fuck up and go to bed, and I told him that this is my fucking house and I am not going to bed unless he answered my questions. So he slap me, and then he drag me down and tried to put his dick in my mouth, I struggled and cried for him to let me and stop hitting me. So I let him put his dick in my mouth, and when he released himself in my mouth and went to sleep, I gave him a nightmare that he will never forget. While he was sleeping, his head was bleeding from the numerous of hits I gave to him from a bat. Then when he came to, he discovered that his dick was in his pocket, along with taxi fare to go to the hospital." **Anonymous**

Pleasure and Problems with Sex

"Majority of men do not understand what it takes to please a woman. They think that they could just put their penis in a woman, and she is satisfied, that is not the case, at least with me. I want a man to satisfy me first with his intellect, his romance, and his gentleness. Many men do not know that they could have a woman more quickly if they display more kindness, and convey more respect for that woman feelings**." Dawn, age 28**

"I had a man with a very nice size dick, but after thirty minutes, I still was not satisfied. All the huffing and puffing he was doing made me mad, I think he moan more than a woman does. Then he tried to give me oral sex, and he could not even do that right. It is a shame that I can fantasize and get off than by men who think that dick is the shit." **Yolanda, age 37**

"I love sex with my man. I mean he tear this shit up let me tell you. He gives me at four orgasms a night, and when I back my ass up, ladies I tell you, both of my holes is under construction, because my man turn them out." **Jennifer, age 21**

"I love when a man slowing put his penis in me. Then carefully and slowly move in circular motions, and then soon as he hear the change in my breathing, he thrust harder and harder leave me and our be soak and wet, and it is not from the sweat." **Sharon, age 30**

"I hate when I am forced to have sex with my man. No, he does not rape me, however, he just not satisfy me, and prefer to fake it then embarrass him. So once a day I ask him to do something different because he does not last long anyway about ten minutes. So he tried to put his tongue on me, and it did not feel right because he kept biting my clitoris, then I ask him to do more foreplay, and I can say I got a little aroused from that. However, but soon as he put his thing in me, ten minutes he was done, and three minutes later he was sleep." **Katrina, age 28**

"Sex and making love is different, see sex can happen without feelings and making love is an act you have with someone you love or have deep feelings for. Many women feel that sex is a determination for a relationship, and they are wrong. You can have sex with a complete stranger, and he can wear your pussy out, but this mean you are in a relationship him? If women give their pussy to a man that is their business, however, if they start expecting that the man is theirs, then they are wrong. Sex should never be used to be a determination for a relationship. See a man can look good and have all the material things plus the right equipment, but how many women go to bed at night with a man with the right equipment and have his priorities in order and still feel cheated and miserable? The size of a man's equipment is not all that important, because a woman can put her finger in herself and after fifteen minutes she done got off. Sex is a joining of two souls, if a woman lay down with a dog, later she will start feeling mistreated like a stray dog. If a woman lay done with a player or cheater, she is going to feel played, if a woman lay down with a man who cares for her and love her, then that woman is the one who winds up marrying that man. Hoes never get respect, but a queen does. **Charlene, age 32**

<u>Children</u>

"The worst thing of breaking up is the impact it has on the children. I was so hurt by the break up that I refuse to let him see the children, I know I was wrong but I wanted a way to hurt him and make him feel how hurt I was. **Mary, 33**

"Although me and my husband are no longer together, I still let him be a part of their lives. A child need their father, and if he has a chance to do right by them a mother has no right to refuse him the right to be in their lives. It makes me sick to hear that a man has to take a woman to court for rights he was given when the child was created. If a woman has to be taken to court because she refuse the father visitation, then what does have to tell you about the woman? **Angie, 26**

"I refuse the father of my kids visitation because he ain't shit. He does not provide for them, and when he wants to do something for them is when I make him think that he is going to get some pussy. I understand a man is suppose to be part of the children in some kind of way, however, if he is wanted because he has not paid child support, and have not brought a toy or pair of pants, then I feel he gave up his rights. If he can hustle to but weed and smoke a blunt, then he should be able at least to take his kids to the show." **Kussandra, age 28**

"Any woman that refuse a man a relationship with his children should have their heads examine. How can a woman carry a child for nine months, and inform the child that it has a father, then turn around and not let him see the children. Those are some stupid ass women, if you had enough to open your legs to the man, and let him put all of himself into you, and enjoyed it, how can you not let him participate in raising his child? See this is why the world is mess up as it is you do not play games with the lives of children, if you love them and really care for them. Mothers need to understand one thing, the children are here for the enjoyment of the parents, and one parent does not have the right to take away a child's enjoyment because a man hurt them. It is not about the here and now, it is about the children's future, if two parents give them love, then when they are older, they will give love to their children, despite if their relationships fail. **Charlene, age 32**

"Well I must be a ignorant hoe, because I do not let my baby daddy see his kids until I feel it is time for him to do so. He hurt me, and when he cheated with that bitch, and coming home having his dick smelling like that bitch pussy, that is when he gave up his right as a dad and my man." **Kimberly, age 31**

"As much as I wanted to refuse him visitation with his son, I couldn't, because our son need his daddy, and if continues doing right by his son, then

Raymoni Love

I have no reason to break up their relationship. Besides, it is not my place to shut a man out of his child lives, that is his choice to be a part of his child life or not." **Helen, age 29**

Hurting Like Hell

"I can not explain how hurt I was when me and my man broke up. See we had a disagreement with the way my parents was in our business. I do not believe they like him any, because they felt he was not my type, but I loved that man. For a long time I barely ate, I didn't go any where and refused to listen to love songs because they made me cry, I was hurt and I will always because I lost someone who was part of me." **Tyra, age 28**

"I was in a relationship where everything seems like it was so perfect. He treated me good and I treated him good, but we wind up breaking up. Until this day, I ask him why did we break up and he said that if we should separate for awhile, because he needed time to think about how serious we are becoming, and if we were meant to be, it would be. Now I know I am not crazy, but why wasn't he honest with me? Sure I saw some men who look good but I was interested in my man and I wanted to know why he wanted out of the relationship. However, he told me later on that the reason he did what he did, is that he could cheat on me, and it was best that he was honest instead betray my trust I had in him. By him telling me that, me and him are the best of friends." **Tish, age 21**

"I became hurt after I discovered that my man lost interest in me. I did everything I could for me, I even became super freaky for him so he would find some one else. However, he started calling me fat after I had the baby, and I would always catch him masturbating while looking at skinny girls in the magazine. I gave up everything for my man; he wanted a baby so I gave him one. He wanted me to give him oral sex, and I oral the oral on his dick, I even tried a three some, you know two girls and him, and he would not even touch me, he was to busy licking and fucking her. He even wanted to play imaginary sex, like I am some girl he lusts after and he is one of my fantasies. Then one day he was in our bed with another woman and he would not even stop having sex with her until he came. After that situation, I will never love another man again." **Sally, age 27**

"I have been before, and I did not want to eat or even go to places that reminded me of him. I felt my whole world was dead, and I felt that I was worthless and useless. I never got over that hurt. The reason I never got over the hurt is that I immediately tried to placate my hurt with another man. That was a big mistake, because I tried to everything possible that would insure he would not hurt me like my ex did. However, that was not the case, I gave too much in that relationship that I did not have any thing left for myself. A broken heart is like a gunshot, that if it hits the right spot, it could end everything you dream, and if it just wounds you, than you will live, but living forever with a scar. **Marlene, age 45**

<u>Finding Peace and Strength</u>

"I can say now that I am happy, cause I believe everything works out according to God's plan. I still see the man who hurt me; well I should say men, because it was quite a few. However, I speak to them and I leave the past in the past, because I have learned that my peace does not live in the misery of other people. Now I make myself happy, and buy my own things and yes, I still date. It is not in a woman's plan to give up on love, we have to protect our hearts more and be honest of the qualifications we seek in our potential male partners. Ladies, men can only do to you what you allow them to do, love the men, but love yourself more." **Angel, age 40**

"I am a happy woman, not because I lost a lover, and a friend because I discovered myself through all the hurt and disappointment. I hurt him, he hurt me, and I believe maturity played a big part in it all. See you can be an adult, and be a baby in love. Many adults have loved, but love the way society and television want them and expect them to love. You can not put expectations on men that you as a woman would not accept responsibility for. If you expect him to give you the sun, moon, and the stars, than you need to give him the heavens, and an ecstasy he could never imagine. In the dating game and in relationships, there is only one thing women need to learn, and that is, do not give a dog a bone, if you are not ready to shovel up his shit." **Erica, age 28**

"I broke up with my man, and now I reunited with him. I believe that sometimes you need to walk through the fire, to understand direction. We women hurt men just as much as they hurt us, some of us just get a little absentminded when he gets caught first before you. Accepting responsibility for the direction of our life, rather wrong or right, will hep us ladies strives to be better mothers, girlfriends, and wives. Don't get me wrong I was hurt like hell when my man and I broke up, but I never stop loving me, and that enable me to reevaluate my plans, goals and my love life. I'm no saint, however, I do what many women fail to do after they get hurt, or hurt the man, and that is accept who I am and what I am, and my reasons for choosing a man." **Sidney, age 29**

"I got my hear broke after continuously accusing my man that he was cheated on me when he was away. Although I had no proof, I blame him for what my last boyfriend done to me in my past. I have learned one thing, if you have any male friends, when you become serious with a man, those male friends must immediately take a back seat. I have many male friends, and he has many female friends, however, I start blaming the things that are wrong in our relationship on the friendship he has with his female friends. However, the same things I was accusing him of, I was doing with my male friends. Now I was not having sex with them, but I would let them bring me things and I cannot keep from crying from how I lost a good man because of jealously." **Juanita, age 21**

Raymoni Love

"There is two sides to love, and there is one feeling you receive when love is pure. When darkness fell, millions of us women were getting our groove on with someone loved. However, now that we gotten our hearts broken we women behave like we forgot how to love again. I learn the best lesson from dating and relationships, If you love someone and they break your heart, suck it up, and keep trying love. See, a failed love affair, enables us women, to learn the meaning of love, and the wrong kind of love. It is like qualifying for a race, the only way you would become a strong finisher and a good winner, you have to, at one time or another accept the agony of defeat. Ladies, you cannot have a baby without crying, and you should not expect to have a man, a marriage, or relationships without problems."
Donna, age 37

In Search for Love

"I will never give up on love, I do believe that there is someone for everyone. However, one still has to be careful, because getting your heart broke almost impel you to do something harmful or hurtful to that person. If men and women were more honest of their past, and their feelings, I believe that dating would not be so bad or complicated. If a woman want to give her sex on the first day or the first week that is her business, however, do not be indulging in shameful acts like this and expect a real man to respect you. I wish that I had someone to cook for and hold at night, but I do believe that one day, I will have that right someone and I will welcome him like I never been with anyone before. **Carla**, age 27

"I wish I could find a man who can love a woman like the those love songs use to talk about. You know the kind of love that never grows old, the kind of love that speaks so candidly about trust and respect. If men would understand that there are millions of women that is looking for them and will love them unconditionally, and all they have to do is erase all the pit bull out of their nature, then they will be able to appreciate the women who needs them. I do not care what anyone says, woman needs a man, and a man needs a woman, because no one wants to be old and alone." **Coretta, 23**

"I want a good man, and I am going to continue looking and being careful until I find that special someone. **Michelle, 40**

"I been married for five years, and I love everything about it, even the good and the bad. I have a husband who cares for me and his children, and we do not keep anything from one another, I believe this is the key to longevity in any relationship or marriage. If there is no trust, or honesty, one will never be able to get along." **Julia, age 35**

"I just want to thank God for my husband and children, because they are the most precious things he has given me. I am not going to mention any of the bad times because they are far and in between, and besides, I erase garbage like that after he apologize or when I apologize. See, once an understanding is establish, the subject should be close, and the process of making more good times can ensue. I do not believe one should go into a relationship or marriage expecting things are going to go wrong. Every relationship or marriage should be centered around positively, because when you plant those seeds of doubt and jealousy, you will never be able to uproot them." **Barbara, age 40**

I will like to thank all the women who took the time to express their feelings in bringing a consensus on certain issues of dating. I understand that there is a great need for love in our daily life, family life and on the job. However, if male and females understand that we only live once, and many of us will not have the pleasure of being embraced by love.

However, as human beings I pray that we all can be embrace by love or friendship. Because sharing a song, a story or even a laugh with someone, is a feeling that will impel hearts to continue reaching for that substance that make us all want to be better at giving.

Many Women Wish They Were You

Chapter 11

Tell me, do you have a complete understanding of what love you want in your life and what love you want to give? I understand relationships can be stressful and burdensome, actuating you into thinking, if it is all worth it. I can say that after you got through the first ten chapters, I know you can find in your heart that it is all worth it.

So now, go out and plan your big day and plans for the future with your family, or even with his family. Marriage or engagement is a perquisite that charters a whole gamut of a life fulfilled. In addition, before we move forward, let us retract the piths of the chapters before, so the message can continue to be embedded in your heart and actions.

…A past understanding

There is not a problem knowing and understanding your man's past. I did not mean harbor grudges or certain prejudices. I meant let the past be his past, and understand what actuated him to conduct himself the he does.

…. Be A Lady

You must understand what kind of man you want. If you are living in a situation where you are always unhappy and stress, you must reevaluate your definition of your preference. Please ladies, keep in mind, you cannot lie down with a dog and do not expect to smell like one.

.... ' Player'

You can avoid the man, but not the 'player'. See, everyone must understand one thing, as long as one is single, meaning not married, they are fair game. If you are tired of your heart being broken or your feelings being disrespected, than you should make a man wait until the 'player' in him leaves.

Remember ladies, a 'player' has no patience, a real man does, so if you find individual a little to eager to taste what is behind your panties (or thong), or want to spend what is in your purse, you already know, cause your 'player' alert has inform you.

.... A Mother of All

Ladies do not impede a path of a future with a man who has children, who knows he may be Mr. Right. When dealing with other children by other people, do so with caution, but also with chary. Love a child from your man like it was your own, this is one reward, which may not and give you a standing ovation, or a star on the ground in Hollywood. However, just imagine your soft touch can one-day put a child on a successful course that he or she may receive this escalade, and you will be the one whom they will appreciate.

…. **Your business and their business**

Everyone may need someone to talk to sometime, however, if you and your man can solve things together, no one else should be helping. You cannot please everyone that you like too, and you will not be accepted be everyone you want to be accepted by, however, as long as you are please with you, than maybe the ones you are trying to become notice by should be noticing you. If you respect yourself, that will motivate others to respect you.

…. **Dry throat**

That chapter if you remember explains it all, if you cannot talk as adults, than you should depart as friends or just depart. If talking to yourself bring more understanding than talking to him, than carry on by yourself, before he rubs some of that crazy stuff off on you.

… Damn your stuff is so damn good!

If another is making him feel good, it is because he wants something more, or you need to be more giving. Go all out when it comes to pleasing your mate, because that sexual feeling you keep putting on him will keep the bills paid, it will make him glad to be working, and it will make him so happy to anything and everything for you. So ladies, put that loving on him, cause what you will not do, the other woman will.

… Some time goodbye can mean hello

I know we all wish we could fix the things that are broken in our lives and relationships, however, some time hurt and pain may mean it is time to move on. See, leaving a love is hard, leaving anything that you are so faithfully committed to is hard, however, sometime leaving, could mean it is time to say hello to you. It can mean it is time to evaluate what your life needs, and for you to regroup and go out to achieve it. Some time it is better to love from a distance, than to feel unloved up close.

… It is all about you

Please women; do not forget about this chapter. You are that priceless gem that man needs to live. You women, who love us and support us when we need it, is that vitality that impels us men to be great. Please continue to be great mothers, doctors, lawyers, mayors, governors, or career orient women, because without your contribution to make this world great, we men would have destroyed it by now. It is important women that your role as positive women must continue to render positive attributes in our world. Remember life comes through you, and cannot be created without you, so carry on and be that lovely source that illuminates a world who so desperately needs it.

When He Says, "I Will"

You have your man now, and you two have survived the turmoil and stress that threaten your love survival. Many women wish they were you, so you have to take the time to really focus on giving your love to one man that many women wish they had. In addition, your man is not perfect, and he is not a mind reader, however, you stood by him so he must be someone special, and that is important. Love is a beautiful and wonderful thing, and to bad, many women have not experience what you are experiencing now. You are a beautiful woman, and it is a priority to inundate the world with your beauty and grace. When your man says I do or I will to you, respect what he is vowing in front of god and family. There are far to many people who do not honor the sanctity of marriage or commitment in relationship.

One day the winds of change will enter your relationship or marriage bringing jealous family members, friends, or neighbors. Through it all you and your man must remain firm, because it is your love that you two have for one another that is important. So go on girl and show the world all that love you have, and grasp all the joy that you encounter from the people who can not help but keep their eyes on you with wonderful delight. Remember love has no meaning without faith, and faith has no life without trust, you cannot have one and not the other, you must have both,

Raymoni Love

or what you are trying to build will only fall by the waste side with the 'what ifs', and the 'how comes'.

Part II:

...Sorry women this part is for the men

Now

Men Are You Ready to Find That Special Lady

Or

Enrich The Love That Is Now In Your Life?

Her Past Is Your Future

Chapter 12

When a gardener plant seeds that of roses, daisies, or tulips, he is not expecting daffodils, sunflowers, or lilies to show up. In addition, this has been the related structure of our relationships; the one we commit ourselves to sometimes turns out to be weeds. Many men do not believe delving into a woman's past is important, just long as they respect you however, you have to explore one's past if you want to have a healthy and successful relationship.

Raymoni Love

Now, you cannot judge a book by it's cover, I believe you heard this before, because people do change. Nevertheless, in order to understand what the meaning of the book you have to read it, and if the conclusion of the book is not palpable to your taste, at least you can put it back on the shelf. This is the interrelated structure of life, and this is the code of many relationships, is to shelve what is not needed.

However, we have to keep in mind, people do change, either for the good or the bad, but they do change. In addition, once you become involved with someone, you just cannot put him or her on the shelf likes a book you read. Because a relationship is centered around two individuals (unless *there are children involved*) and when you decide to end any relationship, your feelings is strongly affected like the one you are getting rid of.

This is why understanding your woman's past, would inoculate you from any nonsense or abuse that might resurface when her emotions are high. Many of us love being in love so much that we sacrifice many essentialities just to make things work. Society donned enormous pressure on males to succeed, however, handling the pressure is not the male's problem, not having auspicious parental guidance creates pressure, and a problem all on it is own.

A woman cannot give the right love to anyone, if she does not understand what the right love is. A mother is the first to give a child love, and the mother is the first that the baby loves. Unfortunately, many children are devoid of this kind of love, and it sometime, actuates them to divest from assimilating into a normal and moral society.

In addition, in their quest to be normal or accepted, they find themselves running down life's spiral and intricate roads, just to wind up psychologically impaired. Love can cure many things, accept a mind and heart that is obdurate, and hate filled. It would take more than love to cure a mind with no conscience; it would take a Supreme Being.

Today, many of you men find yourselves in situations where you are questioning your woman and her behavior. It is apparent that many of you men want love and to be treated right, but just cannot erase the fact that your woman is behaving like a damn fool.

A female child not reared in a positive family atmosphere has a deeper pain than the ones that does. Now I do not mean they are inferior or degenerate when it comes to intelligence and social skills, oh no! It just means they love different, and sometimes it may take awhile before they truly and sincerely show it. They are apprehensive, because everyone, whom they ever loved, did not love them enough, left them or took them for granted.

In addition, their behavior may reflect their concealed hurt and disappointment. Nevertheless, they still can love, and as they grow into adults, their hearts always will question love, and the giver of it. So, when you find yourself dating a woman with a trouble childhood, keep these things in your mind.

Your woman relationship with her parents is extremely important when it comes to the development of your relationship. However, children being reared in homes with honor conveyed to them understand that it is imperative that they give it to their own family and relationships.

Raymoni Love

Men please understand that majority of women has a 'panic' room inside of them, just to control, and hide from unwanted dangers. See many of our girlfriends or wives have been sexually abused as a child, either by her parents, family, or strangers. They find it extremely difficult sometime to love or to receive love, cause her violation that happen to her, has abused her spirit, her mind, her heart and her trust in men. The psychological disorder they have impairs their ability to trust us. See, men in order to find the right woman, you have to thoroughly and honestly understand yourself and what you will tolerate, cause women who have been abused, will sometime act out this fear and distrust, with violence or arguing, leaving us tired and ready to retire from the relationship.

In today's society, there is a big misconception when it comes to relationship and who should be in control of them. In addition, with the emergence of women in politics, education, and employment, women have certain ideals that convince them that they can live without a man, and by the way we men carry ourselves, I agree with them in many ways.

See, brothers, we love to induce fear in our women, friends, or children, in order to receive respect. This is very wrong, violence does not induce fear, and violence begets violence and soon destroys the purveyor of it. Sure, our women may nag or say things to belittle us, and it makes you wonder what cave or hole she derive from because we thinks she is crazy. This is when her 'panic' room opens, sometime brothers we have to face the fact that some of our women never receive the right kind of love, so she failed to learn it and she ignorantly cannot give it. Now, do not get me wrong, women to can be violent, and our fear of losing her or going to jail we refuse to strike her back.

Nevertheless, there is a need in every man to have a woman, in this book, you will understand what kind of woman you need, and what kind of woman you want. See; in a woman's past, you will learn if she wants someone to provide for her, or if she just wants us men as friends and not companions.

I was over my friend's home the other day and him and his woman was disagreeing, I believe over who is going to sweep the floor or something, and his woman became violently disagreeable, and struck him over the head with the broom. Then soon as he tries to restrain her, she starts reaching for a knife, and soon as she gets hold of one, he knocks her down.

She gets up and runs out of the house screaming that he was trying to kill her. The neighbors did not know who was wrong, but all they can see is that the man, her man was standing on the porch with the knife in his hand, and that was the story they told the police.

Well, unfortunately, they are still together, and she is still striking him on top of his head with anything she can find. Why do we human beings, perpetuate violence just to persuade another to our way of thinking or our way of life. Still, brothers, if we are the ones perpetuating violence, it is wrong to be striking our women.

Love is kind, love is compassionate, and love is sincere, and if two people have to result to violence to solve their problems, is heading into a future of self-destruction, and one cannot equate this as love, but an emanation from an trouble rearing.

Raymoni Love

I was in a relationship where I almost was violent, women, with a trouble past will express their discontent with violence, and push a man to the limit; the violence I experience in my relationships came as matter of me defending against the violent attacks of that woman.

Violence permeated my childhood and adult life, and no, I am not talking about me being the perpetrator. I have seen women and men in violent relationship, and their fear of being alone is leaving them with a foolish excuse of accepting it.

I believe that eighty percent of men incarcerated is there because of a woman. Women may not have been the participants in the crime, but somehow she was there either in the mind of the deviant, or being attacked by him.

In addition, the fact remains for violent men and women, anyone succumbing to violence to solve their problems is only adding to them. Everyone strives for acceptance and this enable them to reach for the highest in employment, sports, and life. However, if you are reaching for the highest fulfillment in your relationship with your woman, you will need the sincerest cooperative understanding of your woman's past from her.

If you are developing deep feelings about a certain woman, in your future, understanding her past will inculcate you on whether it will be a happy future or a traumatic one. If you date a woman and you detect early that she has characteristic of jealousy and possessiveness, save yourself the trouble, and leave her alone. Jealousy is a sign of weakness, and possessiveness is indication of control.

How to Find Success in Marriage, Relationships and Love

You do not need to be controlled or trapped by a woman to be loved. You have your own mind, and even a clone understands this. Men help her to understand you love her, and that you are committed to her only. If she does not get help for her jealousy, frightening temper, or any kind of abuse, and then move on. I know you believe you are worth more than what a careless woman can offer.

However, everyone must reach for the highest heights in life, and having a thorough self-examination, can one truly achieve greatness in life. Help your woman correct her problems, and have her to help you correct yours as well.

There is a great need for peaceful coexistence in relationships, without this peace; there would not be anyone around confabulating on how great pure love feels. Men although we are blamed majority of the time of what is wrong in our relationships, this does not mean we falter on our journey of giving women the greatest love possible. We need to except responsibility for what is wrong and right in our lives, and find the courage to transform our lives positively without falling in the traps of the wrong woman.

A Lady and Her Opposite

Chapter 13

When I started dating, I could not believe all the bullshit that was in the dating wold, and after I got my feet wet, I repeatedly kept choosing the wrong woman. Now I wondering was my bar I set for the right woman was too high, or did I have the right qualifications set, just all the nice breasts and asses just made me forget what I truly was after. Men, our eyes are like radar, as soon as we see something of our preference, we either freeze up (*for some of these brothers*), or we go in for the kill. As teenagers, we knew what our preference was for looking for women, whether it was out of immaturity or not, the ideal remain imbedded in our dreams until we reach a more mature age.

In addition, the dating game has provided many concerns when one is searching for love, one has almost have to numb his feelings just to discover the right love for them. However, our task may seem difficult and frustrating, but this does not compare to the heartache we will receive if we men do not take precautionary procedures. We men associate with our buddies and discuss politics, sports and women, and we always deliberate on our present women or our preference, however, the issue remains, what kind of woman or what kind of woman you prefer? 1) A woman who wants a career now and family later.2) A woman who already has children and want more. 3) A woman who only wants a sexual commitment, and the list go on and on.

In addition, we still have that choice, what is our preference when it comes to our hearts.

Some of us men have women in our lives that are the complete opposite of what we prefer, and some of us who are living with the wrong women in our lives are inducing unwanted stress and heartache. Yes, I know we men are strong, virile and confident, however, no matter how masculine and virile we are, a simple heartache will knock you down on your knees or drive you to death. Yes, heartache will kill a person slower than a bullet, but with more endless pain. Life is one big game show, and as one explore its contents, he becomes bewildered, because he has no other alternative but to play.

In the love's game, you may have numerous choices of which you choose to love; it is just a matter if you will make the choice for sincere attributes or for physical attributes. So now, let us bring out contestant number one, she is from a state called 'no damn good', so she is a citizen of 'no good'. You may have a woman that has attributes like woman, and you may have deep feelings for. However, a woman who is considered 'no good', may, or may not have any goals that she is trying to achieve. She doesn't cook or clean, she doesn't keep herself looking good, she either smoke marijuana or some other drug, her children hygiene and clothes are soiled, she doesn't understand the meaning of keeping a clean house, and she gossip all day while she watch the soap operas. Tell me men, is this your preference for a woman.

Now she may love you, and you may love her, however, after reading this book and **(What Is Wrong With My Man?)**, no one whether they are male or female, are going to tolerate anyone with these pathetic attributes. You come home from work, and her face is glued to the television, no dinner is cooked, and only delight she have for seeing you is asking you, "…. did you bring any cigarettes home? Your children or her children are up screaming and shouting like school is something like an unidentified flying object standing on an imaginary foundation, depressing is not it? Yes I know, no one wants to come home to a fiasco like this, well brothers, there are plenty of men who come home to this type of women everyday of there miserable lives.

In addition, after you discover that you do not have cigarettes, you try and lay your tired body down, she comes into the room screaming and arguing with you on why are you laying down, or she may start an argument over something futile. However, an argument ensue, next thing you know you two are spitting out names like bitches, mother fuckers and hoes at one another. Then you become so enraged you have to go out and get a beer or something just to calm your nerves, to no avail, you're now depressed, wondering how can you live with this woman and why did God put you in this situation. Then before you know it, her friends are on the telephone, your woman is screaming to them of how she should put your ass out and find her another man. Men, this kind of woman, need to have a sign on her back that says, "Avoid with Extreme Caution."

Now here is a woman who have made you a sucker, or is making a sucker out of many of you men, she is more of a wreck of a woman, she love her some sex, and will do anything to get it. She plays stupid ass games about commitment, and want you to buy her this, take her here and take her there, she want money for this bill and that bill. Sure she'll give you plenty of sex, and she'll blow the tip off your penis, however, if your money is not right, or your car is not right, she will move on to the next sucker.

Here is a woman, who is one of the worst kind of woman you can encounter, because you never know what her goals are, you do not know her sexual background. In addition, her life could be filled with violence and drugs, and I know it is not a pleasure to put your penis in a jadish female who another man just satisfied twenty minutes or ten minutes before you. This woman, will destroy many of you inside out, when you think that she is capable of love and capable of giving it to you, you'll soon discover, that you're nothing but another man whose blood flows to his penis when she puts her mouth or body on it. Sure you may feel nothing is wrong with that, just ask a man who had a woman who he felt was his but wasn't, he either killed a man over her, or he almost got himself killed, and besides women like these could give a damn about sexual transmitted diseases.

Let us move onto another woman, she is a woman who is making it but is struggling like many of us with life and life intricacies. She is a normal woman with goals and aspirations, she may be in school or some institution of learning, however, and she is trying to make her ends meet. I know what you may be thinking, "What is wrong with this woman?" well let me highlight her shortcomings that may be a little too much for some of you. Her shortcomings is that she have been hurt and mistreated in her past, and she is a little untrusting, so she does not want to be bothered by men at this time. Some of us men may see these attributes as trouble, and we have the chose to deal with them if we choose to, however, a woman who is a regular independent woman persistent in her endeavors to be something positive is a woman I would not overlook.

Though she may be untrusting due to her past, however, she once was a woman that had a job or was going to school, and still made time to take care of her home and man. Men if have a woman who has attributes like this woman you better hold on to her and treat her right. See the woman I am talking about is a homemaker or is in some positive occupation, however, her health is good, her spirit is good, and her character is good. The homemaker of a woman has your dinner ready and bath water ready when you come home from work (now men we must be able to do the same for her as well). She have the children or the home looking immaculate, she may or may not hang out with her girlfriends, however she let them know where they stand. She comforts you when you are down, and yes gentlemen, as she will give you a little hell when she thinks you are fallen from your elite status. A woman like this is a gem, men, are you man enough to appreciate her

    Repeat with me gentlemen, "do not be discourage by a successful woman," jus go out and get her. However, just make sure your priorities are in order, cause success loves success, and if you do not have it, you need to be on that road that leads to it. Whether as a doctor, lawyer, teacher, beautician, factory worker, or just an woman doing the best that she can, they all value love, we men must make the decision, if we are ready and give it to them.

Raymoni Love

You do not want to be an old man wishing for some young tender to massage your limp, women love change, and are continually changing for the better, even Viagra couldn't give you a lift when women looking at you as a underachiever.

She Can 'Play' Your Ass As Well

As You Can 'Play' Hers

Chapter 14

I have been 'played' by many women, and I know many of you have to. Women are the true 'players', and the originators of the trend. See women had to use what they have to get what they want. Back in prehistoric days, I'm sure when she became tired of a cavemen pulling her around by her hair, she just simply gave him some of that cave woman's juicy hot dirty sex, and as soon as he went to sleep, she clubbed his ass to death.

Prostitution is the oldest profession, besides lying and stealing, and women who had other responsibilities, had to play emperors, Kings or even Queens sexual play toys. In addition, women is not going to be with a man just to be with him, he has to have something to even make her considered talking to him, like looks, hygiene and conversation, and let us not forget finance.

Women of today have became wise as far as the dating and relationship game is concern, and they are tired of being wives whom is taken for granted, so they have developed a technique, and that is to find a sucker with money. Some of you who are reading this book are because you want to honestly know what is wrong with your woman. Just ask yourself, when you met or meet a woman what are your attentions. Was it to just get sex, money, or companionship?

Now, how many of you men had women when you found the woman you decided to be with? That woman you left behind are the same woman with a different motivation that is 'playing' those 'other' men who are also reading this book. In the relationship game, many of us have adopted the first strike capability, whomever can get what they need first, must get out before their heart is tied down. However, we foolishly mistaken the facts, we must stop thinking that we can continue to mistreat these women and nothing is going to happen to us. What affects you directly affects her indirectly, and one of you is not going to appreciate the rigmarole that is coming via mail on your doorstep.

See we men walk around looking at women with their big Asses, pretty ass breasts, and lovely faces, our dicks immediately get hard.

However, women walk around with the same ideal, just different sexes, looking at our looks, our wardrobes than his bulge in his pants. Many of us has been 'played', we have taken a woman out and gotten her flowers, clothes etc., than she continues to put us on the back burners, have us in limbo, wondering if we are going to get our 'nuts' out of the sands. In addition, when she gives us some loving, we start feeling this could be the woman you want a relationship with. This woman can be everything to me; however, this is where we go wrong. See, we are making the same mistakes as Samson, I know you remember this strong fellow with all the strength a man can possibly have and fall victim to a hot whore on a camel.

See Samson was a man who was given massive strength for carrying out the will of god. However, when you hear of the story from others the main thing you hear is how strong he was and how he was 'played' by a woman with bad intentions. Nevertheless, this is the most essential and honest truth of how a woman can destroy a man with empty promises and words.

Samson believing that he has found true love, only to discover that he was destroying himself by putting his heart and faith in a woman, that later he would have to kill himself to extricate himself from her grasp. This is why you must love yourself unconditionally first, and give love to a woman who you know is well deserving of it. I believe deceit is spread by mistreat, women and some of us men mistreat one another, because we have not truly understood our past pain, and have not forgive and move on.

Yes, women can be no damn good; however, they became this way, because some of you no good ass men made them that way. Some man in

Delilah past have used her and mistreated her, so now the only thing she knows that will counteract her lost and pain, is to deceive the average man who thinks with his dick first and heart second.

When we decide that a woman could be our main women cause her pussy is good; we are making terrible mistakes before establish a true foundation. By committing ourselves to this hopeless and unwise ideal, we are inducing vulnerability, hurt and pain in which we'll be needing another version of this book, 'What The Hell Is Wrong With My Woman Again?"

Yes, women make the same mistakes, thinking because we sex the hell out of them, that we must now be their men, hell no! When sex becomes a determination for a relationship, than what relationship do we really have? It is not how big a man's penis is or how good a woman's vagina is, it is how good one's heart is.

Why do you think you can be with your woman for years and make her scream how good your dick is, than before you know it, someone else is hearing the same thing, only it is coming from your woman. I have seen a woman having men bringing her food, money, and even been given a car to drive, still 'playing' the field. If she give a man oral sex, you won't know it, if she have sex with another man, you won't know it because vinegar and water can tighten it back up.

A woman has needs, and if we have what she needs, than some of us men have to sometime play the sucker. Men do not think that you are going to just have sex with her and push her to the side, and come back when your dick gets hard, oh no! Because before you know it, you will be paying her rent, car note, and buying her time and senseless affection.

In order for us men not to be 'played' by a woman, you have to make her understand one thing first, "I love me", I love my hard earn money", I love my time," and "I love my sanity." Do not play games with these women wanting to be 'players', tell them school was out for you a long time ago. If these 'player' women want a man for material things, tell them the corner is always free for them to stand on, so they could be easily compensated for their shameful acts. Just keep in mind gentlemen, if you go in a relationship buying, than expect to come out crying.

In addition, we men have to be careful of a woman's greatest strength. A woman can throw that math on us so damn good; you will want to give up your citizenship. Also, do not fall for their sad ass stories or lies as well, a woman can run down lies so well, even her God will believe them. So, if you do not want your heart broke, then do not go broke trying to please a woman. Whatever you are giving her that you are not giving yourself, than maybe you need to see a priest, well maybe not a priest, but a psychiatrist. However, a woman can break a man down so bad, that even his soul would not want anything to do with him, so he just might need that priest.

The dating game need a transformation, because no one believe that they can find love in a relationship, and disappointments and heartaches occur in the dating game, is the understanding of respect is not practice. Men if we want to find that queen that impels us to be better men, better husbands, boyfriends, we need to reaffirm our belief and commitment in making love believable. So, in order not to be 'played' by these women who have nothing but bad intentions covered up with certain niceties. We need to keep our mind off just getting some 'pussy', and put our mind on conserving the ideals of the men who are genuine in establishing the true meanings of love. Therefore, men, please keep in mind, that suckers are 'played' real men get married.

Your Woman, Her Friends, Her Family

And You, Her man

Chapter 15

There are numerous of problems that can impede the progress of a relationship, one of them is outside influences. I fervently believe that opinions that are not guided on wisdom and positive concerns should be silenced. You have your woman and she is taking care of her responsibilities as a woman, however her family and friends are in the mist of your relationship.

In the past, it was respectable and beneficial to seek approval from your woman's parents, and since everyone loves to be accepted, you as her man must understand, acceptance is something one must not be concern with. Honor has always come to one who approves of their moral and intellectual concerns.

I use to try earnestly to be accepted by my ex-women families, because I really wanted them to feel that I really cared about their daughter. On many occasions I just was not accepted, they felt that I was a nice person, however, just not nice enough to date their daughter. Soon this would later put a terrible strain on many of our relationships, because my women would try on several occasions to convince her family that I was a good man, and to no avail, her plea fell on obdurate hearts.

When she go to visit them every time she comes home, I would drill her with questions about what was said about me, but every time I came around her people, they would hypocritically behave like they were happy to see me.

See, every relationship goes through problems, and sometimes we need someone to share our problems with, someone who is less expensive than a psychologist and more honest than our families.

Your woman may be close to her mother, and her mom may not approve of you, neither one of you should let anyone put a stain on the relationship. She must be willing to ask her mother or father for advice, and if it is pleasant or negative she must discern it apply the positive to his life, and then move on with her life. Gentlemen, please understand, when you try to impede the advice from the one person who is close to your woman, you are asking her to give up her confidant and later on, you will be asking her to give you up as well.

Sure, family should mind their own business; however, you are in love with their family, so it is there business, especially if she decides to where you are a ring on her finger. Yes, it may become rough along the road, and it will seem like they are questioning your sincerity and integrity, you must never put yourself in a position to abdicate your morals, if you are a real man, be one. Your self-respect will generate so much acclaim that just when they feel that they do not approve of you they will wind approving of you.

If in-laws are like out laws, and then some friend s must be like crack heads, never having the right thing to give, but always asking for it back. If your woman does not disassociate herself from negative friends, what does that say about your woman? Sure it is all right for her to go and hang out with her friends, however, she must separate her friends from her relationship. I know some of you men have someone who you can sit down and talk to whether it's family or friend, like I said before, if you are going to discuss private details of your relationship just make sure it is not going to be expensive.

See some people who you may consider a friend or maybe someone in your family you trust could be the one who will put all your personal business in the streets. A king will not jeopardize the success of his kingdom by consulting with fools, and your man should not jeopardize the success of your relationship by disseminating his personal affairs with people who does not have her interest at heart.

In addition, you should not interfere with her relationship with her family or friends, she is a grown woman (at least I hope she is) she is capable of making decisions of her own. You are her better half, so if she is complicated with a problem you will be the first to know. Men please understand every woman needs to get away from home for a while, you may not be to particular of her friends, but they are not for you to choose.

If there are children involved, it is great to have both families participating with the children, however, when it comes to welfare of the child no on should be closer than the mother and father. I am sure some of you men have discovered everyone wants to give advice on your child and how to raise it, I know this can be difficult and painful. This is when you must put anyone one in there place, whether it is your family or her family, if you two are doing a good job with your children, than those outlaws need to find them some other business.

You are her man, the pride of her life, you come first, and the families come second. Do not be that fool running around town trying to please everyone that you can. You will wind up destroying yourself and those hypocritical people will only say that you shouldn't have ran your self in the ground, even though we know it is them who are trying to work you in their 'family'.

So, gentlemen remember that you only go around this earth one time, give your woman all the love that you can, respect her family and friends and you will discover, being yourself is a wonderful transformation. Than one day, those who does not approve of your wonderful qualities, will one day wish that they have them for themselves. Be the rock of your own family, your woman, your children, and yourself, because through it all, this is where your love will be greatly honored.

A Father of All

Chapter 16

Through the vistas of time, mankind is continuing to ignore the fact that we are one big family. One day, when occupants in relationships begin to understand love, that will be the day, when heartache will not exist any more. However, in today's society, we men are responsible for other men irresponsibility, and vice versa. Our women are demonstrating to us their ability to be mother and 'replacement' father, in which they need to be commended.

In the dating game, our preference is high on the perfect list, even though we are far from we insist on dating women who has all the 'perfect' attributes, such as nice buttocks, nice breasts, and a body that signify how she can put it on us in bed. However, we thought of the possibility that we are not perfect, so why should they be.

Relationships success needs the contribution of both parties, and when children are involved our example should be polished with caution, cause now we have other lives than our own that need proper guidance. However, our relationship may begin seemingly perfect, and they never end that way, the children, if there are any, are left with their mothers while we ride off towards child support, financial instability, and to another unwanted woman with children.

Many of us wish not to date a woman with children, cause of baby daddy drama, and the fact of having the responsibility of a young life that may need guidance that we may not be able to give at that time. However, if you want the woman, you must take the little crumb snatches they have, or you should move on if you feel that the load is a little to heavy for you. It is a terrible game we men are playing, we are making babies and raising others. Many of us men have acquired large amount of gray hair from stress our baby momma and ex-girlfriends have taken and are taking us through.

Now, just imagine the stress and uncertainty the mothers of these children are going through everyday while being a mother and father? They have to dress the children for school, cook dinners and prepare them for bed, a task we men should be participating in because the joy of parenthood is when two adults whose is wise and understandable of the toils this life can have on a child.

When we date a woman with children, see some of us ignorant brothers and women want to be 'players', are only concern with getting a piece of ass, and this calamitous trend is destroying the nucleus of our existence. The children may not be yours, however, it is still a child, and unless a community contributes to the care of a child's development, the world in which we live always be in an abyss of violence, drugs and unrest.

It is okay if you decide that you do not want to be their father, if you have understanding, you will understand that you can never take the place of their father. However, you are still a man, and if you care anything about your existence, you would conduct yourself in a moral and dignified manner, so the children could envision a world where hurt and neglect of neglect is only illusionary.

Now, some of us date the women who always be saying things, "My children don't need a father," or, "Just be concern about me do not be worried about them," and we as men must respect their decisions. However, in the inception of any relationship with a woman who has children, if you feel that the chemistry is not up to your standards, and you have grown attached to the children, the idea of wasted time and effort makes a departure so difficult.

Women with children are still entitled to love and respect, just imagine the boyfriends and stepfathers around your children, and shacking up with your former loves. These lovely women open their lives to us, their homes, and families to us, and all many of us ignorant ass men can think of is getting some sex, without having compassion that these women have been through nonsense with their past loves.

In addition, a ready-made family can also be detrimental for us psychologically, because we invest out time and finance. Then soon as something go wrong, the mothers of these children without no hesitation, kicks us out of their homes, knowing damn well we have limited places we could find to live. We men can sit around and buy food and clothes for the children, but soon as we correct the children, we are immediately put into our assigned place. We can ponder all day about how we provide for this ready family, but soon as something go wrong, we are dismissed. These are risks we must prepare ourselves for, however, if love is what you have, or what you two are trying to establish, than proper guidelines must be affix before you move forward in the relationship.

See we men need to understand something, many mothers are already under stress, and they have to look towards tomorrow with anxiety that is always saying to them, "Do I have enough food for my babies, do I have decent shelter for my babies. Do I have enough clean clothes for my babies." Moreover, if they do not, the last thing they need is an ignorant man coming into her life making it more complex and difficult.

    I remember I dated a woman with children; I invested time and energy trying to ensure them that I not only cared about their mother but them as well. However, those children drove me crazy, but I continued along in the relationship, which after a short time the children became exceptive of my presence and settled down a little, however, they still drove me, crazy. I was not trying to be good to them because of their mother had great sex, because that definitely was not the case. However, I was trying to show them that someone do care about them, and that I wasn't trying to take the place of their fathers, even though some did called me daddy, I was just trying to love a child that needed a father figure.

    Men, do not just come into these women's home behaving like you don't see the children, their hearts may be small, but they still desire respect, and it is our responsibility as their elders, to give it to them.

    The relationship we experience with single mothers may be short or long, however, a little understanding never hurt anyone, and one thing you can say for yourself, is that you treated her with respect, and you treated her children as if they were your own. I know we would love to raise our own children, however, we are sometimes put into situations where we have to give love and guidance to other children whose fathers may be to obdurate and stupid to share. The rewards may not be so great, and a thank you may never come, however, your heart and mind can always be overjoyed, cause you gave a child a chance to be welcome and loved in a world and community who may sometime fail to see their importance.

Understanding, Can Be Hard To Come By

Chapter 17

When laughter and intimacy is replaced with screams and 'fuck yous', you realize there is a problem. Everyone enters a relationship with an understanding that each day will not always bring blue and sunny skies. However, you proceed with the faith that you will extinguish any problems that may impede the success of the relationship, only to discover that what you are actually extinguishing is the communication that began the peace process.

Raymoni Love

You want to solve all misunderstandings, only to discover that in our misunderstandings, no one wants to be wrong. You reach a critical point where you are screaming and using vitriolic words, she's shouting just to talk over you, and before you know it, hurtful words and actions ensue, establishing an detrimental foundation that will always be remembered when you disagree again.

It is okay to disagree; it is just how you disagree which is important. When there are two people talking at the same time, who is doing the listening? There are several things, which can test the strength of a relationship foundation. Whether it is financial, instability, employment stress, or family issues, problems arise and adult situations cause for adults with understanding. Communication is what keeps love and understanding present in pressured situations; however, one must have the compassion to share it with the one they love.

In many relationships, you will always find someone who does not express him or her thoroughly, and this is where things become difficult. In my relationship, the smallest thing I would let worry me immensely. My woman would practically beg me to express what is on my mind; I would shrug her off and just reply that I was not thinking about anything. I wanted to tell her what was on mind, however, hurting peoples feelings have always came difficult for me to do. Than I learned, that honestly may or may not hurt the one in the receiving mode, but it would forever insult the one in the giving mode.

Does your woman have a difficult time expressing herself to you, or do you have difficult times expressing yourself to her? Ask yourself what is it that always has you and her at each other's throat? I will try to cover certain issues that have relationships on the rocks:

Your Words That Verbally Abuse Your Woman

I understand it can become difficult with your woman, who does not know how to respect you. In addition, there is nothing in the world so dreadful and demeaning than to have someone assassinate your character and positive attribute with hurtful words. Vitriolic words will live with you until you get Alzheimer's, and then you might not forget.

Gentlemen, our women are tired of being some man's bitch, some man's whore, and some man's tramp. Sure, we may find ways to apologize for using such words with our women, and may even throw a little sex on them to help clear their mind from the verbal abuse. However, when she does not come home on time, or she does not cook what you want, or she does not give you unlimited sexual pleasure, such as oral sex, then you'll soon rediscover that she is still a bitch or a whore to you.

Your Woman's Words That Verbally You

Now I know our ladies can tear our manhood apart with her tongue. When situations become incensed, that deduce verbal insults amongst you and your woman, we wonder how they find the words, however they must emanate from somewhere on the darkest side of hell. Words like, "motherfucker your dick ain't shit, that's why I'm not fucking you", "you are a sorry ass man, you can't fuck, you can't keep a job, and you're a punk ass motherfucker", and the list of names go on and on.

Now gentlemen, we must understand why common courtesy is so important. If you and your woman cannot talk to each other like adults with wisdom, then you should depart as friends. Majority of problems in relationships arise because honesty and genuine concern is not present. When financial problems surfaced, it will be best if the two of you handle the situations honestly and carefully. One has talk, while the other one is listening and compromise.

Let's say a bill is due, and the analysis discover that someone is spending well needed cash on things that they shouldn't, like entertainment, or you might have spent some on your car, or you she be shopping when actually she should be looking like she is shopping. Understanding where the money is going and coming can give an honest appraisal when financial problems manifest their ugly heads.

Saying I Love You And Showing I Love You

When you love one another, saying it is an indication of truth. See, you can easily tell your woman that you love her, however, if you are not showing it than you do not love her. Action is a language all of it's own, and abuse is a language all of it's own. Showing humility and understanding when one disagree, is an indication that love is present, when communication and verbal abuse is used to explain things that proper English can, than is extremely important that adults put them in there proper places.

How to Find Success in Marriage, Relationships and Love

Gentlemen please keep in mind, you can go around this world telling everyone that you love them, however it will go in one ear and out the other. However, if you find a way to show them in their life that you love them, then the entry into their heart will not be denied.

Why Another Makes Her Feel So Damn Good?

Chapter 18

There are no cures for broken hearts; cause broken hearts never mend when they can always remember. The saddest chapter of any relationship occurs when one decides to solve their discontent of a relationship to cheating. Yes everybody can see that you are a man, so what! Men cry, and there is nothing wrong with it. Why does she cheat? Lovers become unfaithful when things they cannot control become too serious for them to accept responsibility for.

A man needs to look deep inside and ask himself, is he doing the right things to satisfy his woman. Women are different when it comes to the qualifications of a male. Some women want a man with looks, some want a man to have security, some want a man to be clean and some want a man with the ability to sexually satisfy them (can you believe some women want a man with a money, no matter how he obtain it?).

Men, if you want to know why your woman is cheating, or why she will eventually cheat. I will go over four detailed parts that will explain all you need to know on how to keep your woman faithful and committed, unless she is a woman who can handle several of you men at a time. The first topic is

Sex

Sex is extremely important when it comes to a relationship, satisfying each other can open many doors that will eventually lead to some happiness. Some of you men are losing your women to other men because you are failing to satisfy their sexual needs. You can expect to get on top of your woman hump and hump and after two or three minutes you want to stop, leaving her orgasm free. You have to believe that there is plenty of men out here who will satisfy your woman like there is no tomorrow, find out what turns her on and have her calling your name for more.

You have to love making love to your women. I mean loving and having her body so it will be squirting that uncontrollable juice. However, women love oral sex, so men if you feel you're out of practice then if you want to keep a woman you better get back in the habit and give her some oral sex. However, do not be afraid to tell her how you want it, see some of you get tired with the same old positions, a woman want her vagina coughing up orgasms every chance she gets. That means, men you need to go all out with your love making, but what mostly is important, you need to show her respect. See you just cannot come out the blue and decide that you want to have anal sex with your mate. Whatever she feels it is right then that is when it is okay. Do not force anything on her, converse with your woman about certain that you are interested in trying with her, it is best that you both consent on experimenting on new positions. In addition, if your woman needs a little help, just tell her how you want it, than she would not feel that she could not make you happy during intercourse. Appreciate your woman's body; make love to her like you will taste her love again, because you need to understand that by satisfying her you will be satisfying yourself as well.

So men, lesson number one answer is: If you want to keep your woman, make sure you give her plenty of lovemaking, then she'll be too tired to stick to find interest in another man

Paying Attention

Every woman love a man whom they can respect, but what makes a woman respect you men, is the way you carry yourselves. Some of my friends have women whom they always took for granted. Your women may keep you looking neat, keep your dinner well prepared, have your children looking beautiful, and some of you do not give a card, flowers or just a simple thank you. Women love attention, there is no crime telling your woman how good she looks, or how stimulating her mind is, it is the simple things men that keep your lady faithful.

In addition, I do not know how many of you men cook, however, just a little magic in the kitchen will always keep your woman stomach delighted and your body pleased. Societies have pervaded everyone with customs and fashions, however, intelligence is something required, and many of you men are devoid of it. Tell me men, who want a man whose is every word is a foul one, you know the kind, always talking about bitches, whores etc, Character is a prerequisite when dealing with society, and a man with wisdom can achieve more in life with his mind than with his penis. Trust me fellows, good lovemaking is important, however, a man with character and intelligence can make a woman proud enough to show the world her man.

In addition, I still cannot believe we still have women in our society who still does know a thing about etiquette. Do you know how embarrassing it is to eat at a table that is not properly set, and do you know how embarrassing it is to see a man eating at a table in which he does not know what to say, or how to hold his silverware? Perfection is not required, however, self respect permeates your lives men, so strive to be great within, than no woman will have to look inside to define, cause it'll show on your face.

If some of you men are fathers, you have one of the respected jobs ever held, because your example will inoculate the world with a president, king, queen, or emperor. We need you to continue, with little more help, raise our babies correctly and with respect, and your women will proudly be willing to give you more.

Thanks be the glory to a man who has a wife, you truly have been blessed. It is a priority to keep your wife satisfied emotionally and physically. Do not stop spoiling your queen with affection and admiration, show the world that no other female stand higher than her on any ground, Than your woman or wife will not have to look else where to find appreciation.

Physical Quality

I understand that none of you men are trying to become a Mr. Universe, however, eating healthy and living healthy will keep your woman healthy. See, a woman love a man with a nice physical attraction, because this is what she'll be having sleeping with her at night, if your body are not right, how do you expect your women to respect and cherish it?

You do not have to over eat or under eat to keep a woman, whether if you are big or small, love will find you, only if you are proud of your physical shape. With all the clothes, they have on the market today, why not introduce your self to them. The reason I'm saying this is because when I'm out of shape, I feel bad and that evokes me looking bad, men we have all the right equipment, please put them to use before the rain of cancer, overindulgence and unhealthy eating rust them out.

Compatibility

    Love is a special thing when one can share it with another; however, one must be willing to accept it in order for it to be appreciated. I know none of you men want your women to leave, however, if things are not right between the two of you, one of you are going to leave anyway. Sex is important, physical quality is important, and personal attribute dealing with quality is important, but if one is not compatible then you must correct the flaws and continue to love. I love a woman who I can communicate with, cause then I am confident that our misunderstandings will be resolved. If you feel that your woman's peculiar ways are not up to your standards, you know what I am talking about, staying out late, and lying, nagging. Than I know there are plenty of women who will just love you to hold them and getting her wet.

    If you do not like taking her out or spending quality time with her away from the home, then that man who you thought couldn't get your woman will. Sharing quality time together is extremely important, and she must be willing to sacrifice too, to keep your relationship amicable. Now you have an understanding of why your woman cheat, all you have to do is follow these guidelines and she will be a good girl and stay home.

    However, if she still wants to mistreat you and cheat, all attributes you have learned will be right and beneficial to your new woman. Never stop loving, because one day that love is going to be accepted by someone who is going to truly and sincerely appreciates it.

Cooperation and Understanding:

Measuring Your Manhood

Chapter 19

"I wish we could just get along," do you find yourself saying this after you and your mate have had a quarrel? Do you find yourself searching deep within for answers that will conciliate and renew your relationship? Alternatively, do you find yourself in a tug of war that has you pulling for a renewed love affair, while the other is pulling for a departure? Then there are those feelings that take you back when love was painless and little less complicated. You reminiscence about the time you dated and fell in love. Your dreams of a beautiful home and family just pervade your mind that a smile unnoticeably appears on your face.

Then reality sneaks up on you, love does not love, and a kind word seems to resonate as vile and loud signifying that your relationship has gone bad. I love being in love. I love everything about love. In some of my relationships, although I saw the signs of it going bad, I would try to make it work. Certain relationships I wanted them to last because of the sex, and the others would be because of the children.

When you are in situations like I was, trying to fix something difficult with the wrong tools, you are asking for stress, distress, and heartache. Though things are not right in your relationship, there is an unrelenting power within that actuates you to go on. Relationships sometime can be a pain, and they can be a joy. It is not so difficult to end a relationship when two people are just involved, but when children are present, many of us have not learned to walk away without vexation or vindictiveness. When I love you spoken by loving lips turns into I hate you spoken by vindictive lips, and with children witnessing the altercation, the altercation is no longer between adults. Children are the innocent little bundles of joy that are unfairly used to make any fight an unfair fight. Children can become uninviting guests in a terrible situation where their parents are expressing conniption and violence. Relationships sometime can be a quest down a road that leads to fulfillment or disaster.

Today's relationships you have couples that have not learned to disagree, and this has become disastrous for the children. If fathers and mothers could display the same courtesy and respect towards each other when they were dating, then their children would still be reared with love, which is so important to their development. The problem with mothers and fathers today is retaliatory responses. The mother's retaliatory response when a relationship has ended is to withhold the children from their fathers, and the father's retaliatory response is to stop providing and visiting the children.

Every relationship does not go through these problems, but in some way or another, everyone emotionally or physically express their dissension for broken dreams and a broken heart. Women are the lovely creatures who share man's rib. I cannot express in words what it feels like making love to a woman who is unconditionally in love with you. When a woman loves you, her sun has your face on it, her dreams are of you, her body has your scent on it, her mind got you on it, and her touch is that of an angel and her eyes is brighter than all the stars of the universe. They say when a woman loves a man, he could be standing in the pits of hell, and his mind could be preoccupied with drinking water or dying, but the moment he is touch by his woman, he is reassured that every thing will be fine. That is love.

When we love our women I mean truly love our women, we would relinquish our last breath just so she could live. When we love our women, the only world that exists is the world that we have built around her.

It is obvious that some of our women have a tendency when hurt to try to punish us men in ways one could never imagine. Yes, we men do our women wrong sometimes, physically, emotionally, mentally and spiritually. This does not mean they should keep our children from us when you they upset. Women do not understand it is not only the man they are hurting but also the children. I was in a relationship where I hurt the one who loved me. Many of us men want love and a beautiful wife, but when we have these things, we still go out looking for more gratification.

We need to understand that when our women are hurt, she has many tactics to use to retaliate. She could dishonor herself by having sex with someone just to get even with us, she can become so incensed and kill us, she could have us killed or injured, or she could just withhold our children from us, and many more. All of this is nonsense, and we need to start behaving like real men in times when you and your ex start fighting and disrespecting each other and dragging the children into it. Do not we know that we are perpetuating an outcome where our children will suffer from neglect and become psychologically impaired? Just because a relationship end, that do not mean we start treating our women and wives like we never cared. Broken homes do not have to scar our children, just because we are not under the same roof together we still should be able to raise our children.

We men we need to stop our rigmarole as well, sometimes we sit back and stop taking care of our and children, thinking we are repaying the mother back. No we are sealing our own damnation. Many of us become 'sucker struck', meaning we want the woman, and even though we aren't with them, we do not want them to move on with their lives. Some of us men start stalking them, harassing them on their jobs, and calling and cursing them out. Some of our craziest and malevolent men want to retaliate with violence and shoot up our ex-mates homes and putting our children in harm's way, if we honestly look at ourselves we would see how bad we really look.

Loving someone is a beautiful thing, but we can still love our former significant others without being part of their lives. Men we need to start taking more responsibility for our actions. I know many of us want a family, children and lovely wife, every thing is not perfect; every rainbow is beautiful but not eternal. Showing love to our former girl friends and wives will result in one the most beautiful chords ever played by a musician. Love women like one would want someone to love our daughters; we must not be blind and hypocritical. Some time us men do you women terribly wrong. We all need to take a course in love and respect, because it is apparently clear we do not understand what it means to love and love unconditionally.

We have to keep in mind, children are the focal point of our lives, if we cannot show them that peace and understanding is the best thing to have, how can we expect them to build a world with these attributes?

Men:

Everything Will Be Alright

Chapter 20

There was never a King who ever reigns that did not find joy in being a father. I take great pleasure in the name father; it just does something to me when I hear my children call me daddy. There are many misconceptions about men and their inability to stand up and be responsible. Society puts enormous pressure on men to succeed. Whether it is in employment, family, or education, man is to express his masculinity and mystique through success. Moreover, when he fails to reach the heights expectant of him, he is look upon as lazy, narrow minded or opinionated.

However sharp the criticizing or dull laughter men receive from their peers when they fail, men can only silence them through success. Every night at the end of his day, men who are unemployed or trying to support him and family, cannot wait to sleep the problem stricken day away.

Life sometime can be hard as crucible steel and you cannot wait for it to change. However, sometime, problems in life seem to inconspicuously ease into our lives leaving more problems for you to endure. There is something going on in our world, whether you're in China, Israel, Africa, Canada or the United States, men all over the world are doing extraordinary things to make this world better.

Nevertheless, they are facing insurmountable odds, because everyone does not believe in freedom and peace. The world is full of man made problems, but man has not digested the idea that only man has the capacity to change the problems, but the question is, do we have the will. The problem is not effacing our problems; the problem is that man keeps creating new ones.

Before we put the world's problems through a microscope, let us focus our attention on certain calamities that occur before we leave our front door. One of the problems is our dedication to us. Man has an inner strength that can have him reaching exorbitant heights, or sinking to lowest lows, if he does not use it wisely.

Men have goals that he sets for himself, but having the expertise to reach them has become man's handicap. I have experience numerous of problems in my life, if I had had wisdom in half of them, I believe my success would have came sooner. We have to understand as men, we are look upon as leaders, and every decision we commit ourselves to, the world opinions will make a mockery of it or have parades in the streets.

We receive the same welcome in our homes, if we provide security and harmony; our wives or girlfriends would let everyone know how great her man is. We thrive for this adulation; praise is something of a vitamin to our ego. However, we have to receive this praise like we necessary deserve it.

In our family life, we have to come to terms of how we treat our loved ones. Neglect is a poison that has furniture filled homes echoing for someone to occupy them. Do you know we sometime enjoy our home, family when we are not there, but the problem is we enjoy it too much, and this is the problem?

Many of us may have someone in our lives, but still feel lonely as raft in the sea. Yes, something is missing. In addition, we, the men of the world, the pillars of strength with all the answers, are look upon as having all the answers.

Sometimes we do not have the answers but pretending like we do, only bring more turmoil. Men we need to get our family together. We need to love our women more, and we need to love our children more. If we feel, our relationships are filled with warmth and enriching, then we must repair any problems that may occur.

Do not get the idea in your head that your company and children will always be there, you could not be more wrong. If you are not giving your women the love, she requires, and satisfying her intellect as well as sexually, then another man will love to take your place.

Yes, some of your women may be difficult and misunderstanding sometime, however, your obligation is to yourself first. If something or someone makes you feel that you cannot spend another day with, then you need to remove that person from your life. Nowhere in the Bible or Quran, does it say that you have to be miserable.

In addition, keep in mind sex is a major part of a relationship. However, it is not the soul part. Women need to feel good sexually, however, they need to feel loved, they need to feel worthy, and they need to feel needed.

Our beloved women are the ones that sooth us when the pain of the world came down on us. They are not involve with us for sexual gratification, or to wait on us with hand and foot, their destiny is tied up with our destiny, and life will become more complicated without the love and support from our women. Nevertheless, she has to be the right woman.

The most essential part of a woman is how she carries herself with dignity and self-respect. In addition, she has to be a good mother to her children. Then it is mainly about what you prefer. If you want a woman who criticizes and love violence (because there are many women who feel they should be the man in a relationship) or hangs out all night with her girlfriends, then do not complain when receive what you ask for.

Do you want a woman who disrespects you by being with another man? Alternatively, do you want a woman when every time you turn around she has drugs or alcohol in her hand? Having the right person can be easy, if you are the right person.

Moreover, for the man whose heart is filled with jealousy and insecurity? We have an issue that we strongly need to address, this sickness is having us doing immoral things that is leaving innocent people dead and landing us in prison. If you feel that your wife or girlfriend is unfaithful, then you need to address your concern to her, and find the truth.

See, a woman can be the most mischievous person on this earth, and will take years before you will discover this. She can play with your mind like she is playing hopscotch. She can jump all over your heart and ego, and jungle numerous of other men at the same time. Just try to give your woman the best love you can give her and if this is not for her, then it will be beneficial for you to let her go.

However, if you do let her go, respect your decision like a man. Do not be calling her twenty times trying to find out if she is with some another man. Do not be showing up at places that are familiar to her, just to see her, and do not be slashing tires and busting out windows. Accept your loss and move on.

Remember one thing about women, they love security, she loves strength, and she loves intelligence. The only woman, who does not like these attributes, is a woman whose personality is void of these things. Upgrade your personality to include these attributes, and when you obtain them, find a woman whom has them.

There is no opposite attract, you will never find a king loving a queen that is not compatible for him. In addition, the most important thing, talk to your woman. It is not about crying or belittling you. Talk to your woman, because if she trusts you with her heart, then you need to trust her with yours. Talk to your woman; let her understand how you feel sometime. Communication can impede war, if the two sides agree to be honest.

Now it comes to our children. They are part of us, although the child came through a woman's womb. It is imperative that we be there for our babies. They need us so much to be part of their lives. See being in a relationship or marriage is different from having a relationship with our children. Marriages and relationships can end at any moment that does not mean our fellowship with our children has to end.

Yes, the women that we love may try to attach strings to our children. You understand what I am saying; she will let you she them on some occasions and then jerks them away when you upset her. This is why you must be very careful of who you have children with. The last thing a man needs is to lie down and be bitten by a snake.

No man should have to go to court and let a court system determine when and where you can visit your children. I understand going through all these problems may disappoint you and have you neglecting your fatherly duties. I know by experience. I have been through it all, and I terribly regret having any children by immature women.

However, life goes on, the children are here, and they need their father. In addition, the same goes for you do not turn your back on your own future. If you have to pay child support, try to pay it, and if you are having a hard time paying, let the court understand your situation, and try to give something (because you and I know a woman will try and get blood from a turnip).

Then ask a social worker of the state to monitor your child support so everyone can see that the child is getting the use of your money. See some women will take your money, get her hair and nails done, or she might use your money on another man. You know how 'players' are; they can soothe gold from a leprechaun.

However, no matter what happens, do not give women the satisfaction of seeing you weak, or not being a good father. Do your best, prove them wrong, and at the same time prove to yourself, that you are responsible. Whatever the highs and lows of your life, always remember do not give anyone the satisfaction of seeing you fail. Do not give up!

In addition, for the men who are in the grasp of the law, everyone is not perfect. You may have done a crime, and is now paying the price for it. Remember that justice is indivisible, and your injustice is a threat to everyone, everywhere. However, you are still a man, accept responsibility for yourself, and strive to be a rehabilitated citizen when you are free. I understand your pain is in the dark, and you miss your families and friends.

Nevertheless, you must remember, you hurt and destroyed someone else's family and friends. Forgiveness may never come as swift as your judgment, just keep in mind the world is never to small for people who wants to atone and avert from it's nefarious past.

So men you are the guardians of liberty and justice. Respect your homes, respect your women and children, and respect yourself. When you are out having a good time in the streets or clubs, keep in mind that you have one life to live. Therefore, love your neighbors and respect their life as well; death can never be repaid? Your conscience needs to be at ease, because human life is priceless.

Moreover, most importantly, give the creator his praise; cause when your nights become to dark to see he is the only one who will give you light that will never go dim or out. ***Be careful, be responsible, stay healthy, and stay alive.***

There is a Meeting in the Men's Room

Chapter 21

Hello, and welcome men to a chapter specifically about conversations I listened and witness about women, relationships and love. I wish that many more men would contribute their testimony on love and women, and since they are not here, other men is eager to fill in for them. Although the conversations you are about to read is not that of the author unless where is specified, every one of them deserves every right to be here and taken very serious. In this chapter, certain men may have different experiences as you and I, however they are seeking the same thing, and that is love and peace with our women.

The Dating Game

"I am not going to lie, I am a player, and what makes me a player, is that I am not ready to settle down. Besides, women are so willing to give their panties, how can resist such lovely temptations. See I was in love once, and that woman hurt the hell out me, so I made of my mind, never to fall in love with these stupid ass women out here. I tried dating, and women go from getting to know you and fucking you, to ordering you around like you are their child. Then when you put them in check, than all of a sudden they want to start looking at other men. The hell with the dating game, unless the bitch is fine is wine, there is no way I am going to settle down. Oh! Yea, she also have to have some good pussy." **Willie, age 34**

"I dated this welfare girl before with two kids, you would not believe how easy I got the pussy. I had her doing every sexual thing under the sun to me, and I must admit I fell in love with that shit. Nevertheless, she had many problems, I had to her help with this and that for her children because their father was in jail and I was the only man in their life. The dating game is cool, if you have the patience and are not there trying to mess up women lives. After I realize what sacrifices she was making for me, I had decided to make her my one and only girl. See I am no fool, When I find a good thing, I learn not to let another man enjoy the flavor." **Daniel, age 25**

"I dated this girl who was crazy, I mean mentally disturbed. She was the most begging women I have ever dated, and violent too. She would go into a temper tantrum when I refuse to let her use my car. She would go into frenzy if I ever told her no. She was very beautiful, and her loving was good, however, none of that was worth almost being killed by that sick bitch. I must admit, you have to be very careful about who you date, or you might wind up dating someone turn you to hate them." **Anthony, age 28**

"I tell you, you have men out here, and you have suckers. The dating game is not for suckers; that it is for real men who are mature enough to see a whore walking into his life, and a queen trying to enter his heart. A whore will give men problems, and a queen will give broke and weak men problems. If a man has his responsibilities in order, they will know who they should date, and who they should walk away from. It is okay if a man is just getting some pussy, but if he want a whore, or a tramp to be his woman or wife, then he has a serious problem. That is why this is the dating game, because some women are going to play games, and many men will get played by them. That is the joy of dating, understanding that everyone from women to men, is playing a part in a Broadway play, and you will not learn anything personal about them, unless they know you have something they need." **James, age 35**

"I do not care what any man says, the dating game is like an job interview, with the right qualifications you will get the job, and without the right qualifications someone else will. There should be no one implementing violence when they are dating, if there is a problems in the beginning that is a sign that things are not compatible. Women may play games with us men; however, it is because stupid ass men have mess things up so badly for us good men who are sincere." **Chuck, age 29**

"What can I say, is that I love the dating game. Why, because I have the choice to put up with a woman for as long as I want to, then kick her ass to the curb when she gets on my nerve. I am not a player, however, what is a player, but one who dates anyone he chooses. If a man or female is not married, they have the opportunity to date how many people as they choose, and that is not being a player, that is being unmarried." **Joe, age 45**

Getting wet for the First Time

"Getting all the pussy I can is my life. I went out on this date before right, and I was being romantic, and smooth at the same time. Therefore, when the night came and it seems she wanted to go home, I ask her to stay a little while longer. So I talked, well I did not talk. I lied mostly. I just wanted to see if she would give me some pussy on the first date. Then before I knew it, she was riding my dick inside of my jeep. Now she had little money, and was a college student, so I kept hitting that ass when ever I wanted to, because I knew one thing about women, if I got the pussy so easy, some other player got it before me." **Chris, age 26**

"I dated this girl for about three weeks, and she unexpectedly called me up to come over her house, because her grandmother had gone out of time. I went over there after I have drank gin, and taken all I kinds of pills that kept my dick hard because I wanted to tear her shit up, you hear me? She had some good shit too, and I see why she had men stalking her because she had snapper, and a juicy one at that." **Calvin, age 35**

"My embarrassing moment came when I got some sex from a woman I been wanted for a long time. She came over my house about three o'clock in the morning, and I was expecting her, but the liquor I drank wish that she should of brought two of her because I wanted to tear some shot up. She gets over my house, and started going down on me, and before I knew it, I woke up it was about eleven o'clock in the morning. Then I turn over to see where she was and the only thing that was there was a note that said, '…you should do something about your limp, I did not know that it fell over when it gets pleasure'. I can kick myself for letting that good pussy get away, but I wind up getting some from her anyway, although the next time I would get some from her for the first time, we were on our honey moon." **Leon, age 32**

"I remember dating my wife, well you know she was my girlfriend at the time, and talk about playing hard to get, she played hard to get. I dated her for three months, because I thought she was special and I wanted to show her some respect. Do you know what happen when I finally got

Raymoni Love

some pussy from her, it turned out that she was a super freak? Man, she had straps, whips, handcuffs, and ice. Now, never mind the whips, straps and handcuffs, but what she did with that ice, I knew I had to make her my wife. She put ice cubes inside her pussy and then her pussy would shoot them out like she was pitching for the Yankees. I knew right then, that when I put my dick in her shit, I would be whip for the rest of my life, and I am, going on fifteen years." **David, age 40**

Children

"I do not know why women want to play games with a man with his children after they break up or divorce. I had to take my baby mother to court because she kept refusing me visitation with my children. She even had other men being called daddy by my kids, how sick can that bitch be? I admit, I did do her wrong, but tell me, why when you break up with your woman, that they want to withhold your children from you. You cannot wish that if you had to do it again you would not be bother with women like these, because I believe men like me, are totally responsible for majority of these women changed behavior." **Robert, age 27**

"I cheated on my wife with a woman that was in her face everyday, and my wife may have expected something but never said anything. So one day my dumb ass told her that I had feelings for the other woman, and I slept with the other woman. She forgave me, but my choice regarding my dick, was the other woman, and my wife still wanted to make our marriage work. Then I just made up my mind, and it was a very bad decision on behalf. The times I would pick up my son from day care, she stop that, and even withheld my son from me until I took her ass to court. In addition, she wind getting personal protection orders to try and keep me from coming around trying to see my son. There was an old saying, 'you never know a woman, until you two meet up in court or some kind of litigation. If I had to do it all over again to be truthful, I would keep fucking that other woman, and stay with my wife, because later on, that other woman wind doing the same to me that my wife did, ain't that bitch? **John, age 33**

"When I broke up with my girl, she would do everything do to me, she did and tried. I want to be a good father to my children, but every time I turn around this bitch is always saying what I am doing and what I am not doing. I pay child support, of which is fifty percent of my earnings, and I have to kiss her ass just so she would not act like a damn fool. I believe they need better laws to stop these women from putting children in adult affairs. You know, actions like these coming from women like this who act like they have no sense, make many men not want to be bother with their own children. I know we men love our children, but with all the bullshit, some of us just give up. However, I am going to keep fighting to the day I die, to make sure that bitch does not keep me from my children every time she gets upset." **Calvin, age 40**

Raymoni Love

"I love my children, however I try and direct their paths wisely. My daughter and her boyfriend broke up and for awhile; she kept keeping my grandkids from their fathers. Then I got tired of it, because I know I would not like it if someone would do that to me, and I took the kids over their where their father was myself, and till this day, there is no problems with my daughter and her ex boy friend. I believe many parents are witnessing their daughters play and mess up their grandchildren's lives by not intervening in situations that need a mediator. I have seen Christian grandparents; the ones who go to church four or five times a week, sit idly by and watch their daughters drive their children's father upset or crazy by playing games with the children. I believe the times is changing, and one day women are not going to be able to play games like these with the children just to get back at the fathers." **Roy, age 56**

To Hurt Too See the Bus Coming

"I dated this woman for about seven months, and I always had a feeling she was cheating on me. In the beginning of the relationship, everything was fine and dandy, but what worried me, was the fact that she had many male friends. Now she would swear that nothing is going on, but I kept getting a feeling that she was cheating some how and some way on me. Now I love this girl, she bought me everything she possibly could, and made some pretty good love to me. Then one day she came home from work telling me that her ex boyfriend came up to her job, and wanted the button to his dress suit. Now it is about seven thirty at night in the winter, and I told her to tell him to go to the cleaners to get a new one, but she was eager to go over his house and give back his button. His house was about twenty minutes away, she stay gone for about an hour or two. When she return, I ask her what took you so long, she said he wanted a hug and wanted to take a picture of me on his computer. She must of thought I was boo boo the fool, and then she wanted to break up with me because I suspected something was wrong. We stayed together for about three more months, but the relationship was never the same. I gave her a car to use, and I did every thing I possibly could to keep her happy, I guess it was not good enough. One time she said she was going out with her girlfriends, and she was not going to drive the car I gave her to use because they are going to be picking her up. So I said okay, go on out and have a good time. She never called when she got in that night or morning, so I kept calling her but her voice mail kept coming on. So I used my brother's car and decide to creep and see when and who is bringing her home, and just like I figured, one of her so called ex boyfriend turn male friend was dropping her off. To this day she swears up and down that they were not doing anything, although he kept dropping her off after she leave for a couple of days. I was so hurt by what she did, I wanted to kill that bitch, I mean I literally wanted to seriously hurt that tramp." **Richard, age 31**

"I can tell you I was so hurt that I could walk across the street and not see a bus or car coming my way. I love my wife for forty years, from the time when we were courting until now. Then, when we were about three years into our marriage, she had an affair; this is what she told me, because I did not know until twenty-one years later. What hurt me so bad, was when our daughter got into a car accident, and needed a blood transfusion, I went to give her some of mine, and the hospital said our blood type were not the same, and she did not have her mother's blood type either. I was puzzled and furious. Therefore, my wife told me of the affair, and I thought from that time on of how I could kill her and get away with it. Today, my wife and I never divorced, but we are not together ever since she told me about the affair. I am the only father our daughter knows, because her real father was killed trying to rob a liquor store. I still love my wife, but the thought that bothered me the most, after she had our daughter, she could not have anymore kids, and that hurt me so, because her one and only child should have been mine." **Graylen, age 59**

"I never felt like I wanted to die, until I walk in on my wife having sex with a man and a woman. I grab my gun and I started shooting and answering questions. Although I miss my targets, my life was never the same after that. The reasons she was having sex with those people made me wanted to kill her still to this day. She told me the reasons why she did what she did, is because her girlfriend kept telling her that her man had some good dick and she should try it. It is important to know your woman sexual fantasy, because one day you might walk in the house and a someone else might be giving her pleasure." **Alex, Age 32**

Love is not shown Through Violence

"I use to beat women down for anything. If I seen my woman looking at another man, I would slap the taste out of her mouth, but now I have changed. I discovered that putting your hands on someone, who will support you through thick and thin, makes you lower than a roach. I love my woman, and though she may sometimes go over the deep end criticizing me when we argue, I find other means to correct her. I do not believe real men strikes a woman, before I was not a real man, but when I discovered what I had and loved, I stop my bullshit all together." **Ronald, age 32**

"The saddest times of my life, is when I struck my baby's momma. She was advising me on a certain job opportunities that were presented to me, and when she mention something about her ex, I kick her in the stomach. She did not have to leave me; I left her and got me some help. It is a shame to have men out here everyday who finds that hitting a woman is a good thing. I went and got me some help, and I beg for my girl forgiveness, and she accepted, and now it has been three years and I have not even attempt to put my hands on her." **Jessie, age 35**

"I was living with my woman and we use to just fight, fight and fight. I was tired of fighting her and wanted to leave, but I had no where to go. Sometimes she would start the fight and sometime I would, but I knew this is not what I wanted out of a relationship. One time things got real scary, I was drinking, and she was just talking shit about my dick ain't shit, or that I could not satisfy a mop if it had a pussy and things like that. I got so offended; I hit her in the head with a beer bottle. A woman can provoke a man to a decisive point, but I had to leave her, because I could not see myself looking at her scar everyday. I believe now that there is a solution to arguments and disagreements, and that is understanding and non-violence. **Carlton, age 29**

Through it all, I am Still A Man

"I can say that I tried to be a good man, and a good father, but women with their insensitive bullshit just makes realize that we have a lot to do to repair the ill feelings between man and woman. However, I am going to still hold down my end, I am going to continue to date and fight for joint custody with my children. I still believe in love, but now I know that sticking your dick in a woman does not make you a man, what makes you a man is responsibility. Having responsibility to know who you are dating, who you are having sex with, and who you are about to marry, because heartache and nonsense is something everyone can live without." **George, age 37**

"I was impatient until the summer time came around, because I love to see women in them summer clothes. However, my life has changed now for the better. I am married with kids now, and I find it great joy to love now just one woman. To all those men out there and to those reading this in my man's book, do not let dating and certain women bullshit get you down. Life does get better, and although they might be doing better than you now, do not let them see you down. Men built this world, and women may be here now, but they learned from us, so we have to reeducate them into being loyal and true. If we mistreat women, or let them use and mistreat us, we are fighting a battle, none of the sexes will be able to win." **George, age 29**

"I must admit, I mess up certain situations I should of used my brain instead of my penis. I cheated and lied on a woman who really cared about me, and now I have to pay. I may not like the child support I have to pay, and I may not like having my kids in the home with their mother's boyfriend, but that is the way things goes. If I were not out chasing chicken heads and whores, I would not be in this situation. It is a long road to recovery when the court and women beat you down and mentally, however, life goes on, and you can either complain and die inside, or get up and may life a little better with all your 'new' responsibilities." **Anthony, age 30**

I will like to thank all the men for contributing their experiences, and I hope you men and women got something from this book that will actuate you all into loving and appreciating the ones you give your hearts to. Love and be difficult sometimes, relationships and marriages can be frustrating and irritating however, you have the power and will to make love enrich every aspect of your lives. I hope the married people and the people in relationships gentrify their love and commitment, so the world can see, that

Raymoni Love

genuine love still exist, and it was you who made them realize and establish hope for something so precious many have substituted for lust.

Thank you,

Keep up the love, and down the nonsense

Many Men Wish They Were In Your Shoes

Chapter 22

Tell me, after reading chapter one through nine, do you have a complete understanding of what love you want in your life, and what love you want to give? I understand relationships can be stressful and burdensome, actuating you into thinking, if it is all worth it. I can say after you got through the first nine chapters, I know you can find in your heart to see that it is all worth it.

So now, go out and plan your big day and plans for the future with your family, or even with his family. Marriage or engagement is a perquisite that charter a whole gamut of a life fulfilled. In addition, before we move forward, let us retract the piths of the chapters before, so the message can continue to be embedded in your heart and actions.

…A past understanding

There is not a problem knowing and understanding your woman's past. I did not mean harbor grudges or certain prejudices. I meant let the past be her past, and understand what actuated her to conduct herself the she does.

…. Be real Man

You must understand what kind of woman you want. If you are living in a situation where you are always unhappy and stress, you must reevaluate your definition of your preference.

Please men, keep in mind, you cannot keep a cat that is not trained to keep her tail down. Sure you may have her newdered, however that still will not keep her from being in heat and having her tail up in the air for every alley cat to smell.

.... ' Player'

You can avoid the woman, but not the 'player'. See, everyone must understand one thing, as long as one is single, meaning not married, they are fair game. If you are tired of your heart being broken or your feelings being disrespected, than you should make a woman wait until the 'player' in her leaves.

Remember men, a 'player' has no patience, a real woman does, so if you find an woman a little to eager to feel how hard your stick is, or want to see how much money you can spend on her, you already know, cause your 'player' alert has inform you.

.... A Father of All

Men, do not impede a path of a future with a woman who has children, who knows she may be Mrs. Right. When dealing with other peoples children, do so with caution, but also with chary. Love a child from your woman like it was your own, this is one reward, which may not and give you a standing ovation, or a star on the ground in Hollywood. However, just imagine your wisdom and understanding can one-day put a child on a successful course that he or she may receive these escalades, and you will be the one whom they will appreciate.

.... Your business and their business

Everyone may need someone to talk to sometime, however, if you and your woman can solve things together, no one else should be helping. You cannot please everyone that you like too, and everyone you want to be accepted by will not accept you, however, as long as you are please with you, than maybe the ones you are trying to become notice by should be noticing you. If you respect yourself, that will motivate others to respect you.

.... Dry throat

That chapter if you remember explains it all, if you cannot talk as adults, than you should depart as friends or just depart.

If talking to yourself bring more understanding than talking to her, than carry on by yourself, before she rubs some of that crazy stuff off on you.

... Damn your stuff is so damn good!

If another is making her feel good, it is because she wants something more, or you need to be more giving. Go all out when it comes to pleasing your mate, because that sexual feeling you keep putting on her will keep the bills paid, it will make her glad when she goes to work, it will make her so happy to do anything and everything for you. So men, put that loving on her, cause what you will not do, the other man will.

... Some time goodbye can mean hello

I know we all wish we could fix the things that are broken in our lives and relationships, however, some time hurt and pain may mean it is time to move on. See, leaving a love is hard, leaving anything that you are so faithfully committed to is hard, however, sometime leaving, could mean it is time to say hello to you. It can mean it is time to evaluate what your life needs, and for you to regroup and go out to achieve it. Some time it is better to love from a distance, than to feel unloved up close.

... It is all about you

Please men; do not forget about this chapter. We are the foundation of a family. Our women and children depend on our ability to protect and defend their honor. We must start respecting one another more, that macho shit can go right out the door, and peace is what we need. Anyone can kill, anyone can hurt and abuse, however, it take less energy and less consequences to love and strive for brotherhood.

In addition, we must start being exceptional fathers to our children, they are our future, also we need to start loving our ladies more, come on men, we all know that when we love our women more, our world is so better. So let us commit ourselves to making theirs better as well. In addition, we must set personal goals for ourselves, if we fail to reach for the highest star, than we will always be committed to fall on the hard rocks below.

Many Men Wish They Were You

You have waited for this moment for a long time, but now the time has come. You have your baby; your love, your queen, and no other woman can compare to her. However, now that you have her, do not neglect her, and do not forget the prime principles in keeping her. Sometime life may be hard, and sometime you may feel that you need a blast off to the moon, however, realizing that you now have your queens love, whatever you go through in life she will go through it with you, this is why you made her your number one.

Man men wish they were you, they wish that they could have what you get everyday and night, however, they fail to understand, it is what your women provide when you are on feet or on your knees that make her unequal. You always had ways to solving your problems with your queens, I just hope I shared with you a little more. You cannot have the ship without the mighty roars of the seas, so expect disagreements, however, remember she has an opinion too, and together you both will be able to calm the seas because you both took time to listen to what the other had to say.

About the Author

Raymoni Love is a writer in its purest form, what I mean, is that he is a complete writer. From poetry, music and books, Raymoni Love is a sensation, whose talents will soon engulf anyone and everyone who appreciates great writing.

Raymoni Love has all the credentials to be such a sensation, by the rewards he receives from evoking love, peace, and understanding in everyone's heart and presence he encounters. Raymoni Love is also a loving and dedicated father and wonderful human being.

Printed in the United States
50415LVS00003B/301-324